GLOBE PRESS BOOKS

To: Editor/Book Reviewer

We are pleased to send you this review copy of:

The Body of Light
by John Mann & Lar Short

Date of Publication: November, 1990
Price: $12.95

Direct quotation in reviews limited to 500 words unless special permission is given.

Please send us two copies of your review.

Globe Press Books
3003 Old Yorktown Road
Yorktown, New York 10598
(914) 962-4614
Fax: (914) 962-1580

THE BODY OF LIGHT

Also by John Mann

Rudi; 14 Years With My Teacher

with M. Richard
Exploring Social Space

Students of the Light

Learning to Be

Encounter: A Weekend With Intimate Strangers

with H. Otto
Ways of Growth

Changing Human Behavior

Louis Pasteur: Father of Bacteriology

Sigmund Freud: Doctor of Secrets & Dreams

Frontiers of Psychology

Behind the Cosmic Curtain:
Further Writings of Swami Rudrananda

Also by Lar Short

Way of Radiance

Commuter Yoga

THE BODY OF LIGHT

BY
JOHN MANN
AND LAR SHORT

Illustrated by Juan Li

Globe Press Books
New York

This book is available at a special discount
when ordered in bulk quantities.
For information, contact Special Sales Department,
Globe Press Books, Inc.
P.O. Box 2045, Madison Square Station
New York, NY 10159-2045

First Edition

ISBN 0-936385-14-6
Library of Congress Catalog Card Number 90-82428

10 9 8 7 6 5 4 3 2 1
Manufactured in the United States

CONTENTS

ILLUSTRATIONS

TABLES

ACKNOWLEDGMENTS

The authors owe varying debts to teachers, students, friends and colleagues they have known in their searches through various spiritual traditions.

In particular we wish to thank the following: Pandit Majrani Tigunait for several helpful conversations on the subtle body in Hinduism and prepublication access to his book *Tantra Science and Practice* (in preparation).

Master Mantak Chia for a number of enlightening discussions of Taoist Yoga.

Michael Winn for his helpful editorial suggestions on Chapter Four.

H. H. Dingo Khyentse Rinpoche for the inclusiveness of his being and the universality of his teachings.

And to our root guru Swami Rudrananda (Rudi).

John Man
Lar Short
June 26, 1988

Introduction

Individuals who are seriously interested in spiritual development are faced with a confusing situation. When they try to choose which teacher or teaching to follow, they discover that all of them claim to be best.

In part this situation arises from the fierce competition that exists in the spiritual marketplace. In part it arises from the egos of teachers, who really believe that they, and their teachings, are the best; a view that is greatly encouraged by their students.

If all teachers were similar, one would have a fairly simple situation, analogous to choosing one's physician. It would be a matter of personal preference and of estimating the general competence of the teacher. But they are not similar. Teachers have very different styles and methods.

For example, in one teaching the student is told that it is necessary to stop all thought. In another he is told to repeat a sacred word or phrase endlessly. In a third he will be encouraged to have an uncontrolled visionary experience. How can these varied approaches all be correct?

There are many ways to explain this confusing situation. It may be due to an honest difference of opinion. It may occur because each teaching specializes in cultivating different types of experience. It may be strategic; that is, by over-emphasizing the differences between teachings, they set themselves apart. As with automobiles, relatively minor distinctions can be blown out of proportion in the advertising process in order to sell the latest models. But whatever the reasons, a spiritual "Tower of Babel" exists.

One way to reduce this confusion is to examine various teachings using a general format that applies (in varying degrees), to all situations. In this book a *three body* model will be employed for this purpose. This approach has the advantage of being simple, relevant and widely accepted. In essence, it distinguishes between three fundamental levels of human experience: the physical (including sensation, thought and feeling); the subtle (which concerns the flow of patterned energies within the body); and the cosmic (where all experience is universalized). To refer to each of these levels as "bodies" may be confusing. Only the physical body has a clearly defined form and density. The subtle body has a form, but you can put your hand through it. It does not have density. And the cosmic body is essentially formless, that is, it is everywhere at once.

We can describe the relation of the individual to these three bodies in two ways. First, that they already exist, and the essential problem is to become aware of them. Second, that the physical body exists, but the other two must be developed through a conscious process of internal evolution.

Regardless of which of these assumptions a particular teaching follows, a tremendous commitment and effort is always required of the individual in order to attain their final objective—the conscious functioning of all three bodies in the liberated human being.

In pursuing this aim, the subtle or energetic body occupies a crucial position, falling as it does between the physical and the cosmic bodies. The physical body is the foundation for the subtle.

And the subtle body, as it develops, becomes the foundation for the cosmic.

The title of this book, *The Body Of Light*, refers to two stages in this process of internal evolution. The first applies to the subtle body, which is typically described in terms of the radiance of its colors. The second concerns the final stage of development, when the physical level is totally transfigured and only a rainbow body—a distinct but nonmaterial entity that is free of all physical limitations—remains. That is the eventual goal. But to get there, the subtle body must be activated; a process which is the theme of this book.

All spiritual teachings have something to say about the nature of this process. This book was written to compare their viewpoints. Furthermore, specific practices from these varied teachings will be presented. They can then be tested by the reader who is interested in their relative effectiveness, and who wishes to take a further step in the cultivation of his or her own subtle body.

Part I

The Subtle Body: Background, History and Traditions

CHAPTER ONE

THE RECURRENT IMAGE

The physical body is the mediator of all our experience. If it seriously malfunctions, everything we perceive is distorted. If it is relaxed and in balance, many of our difficulties fade to insignificance. The impact of the body on our awareness is stronger than the influences of history, culture, or psychology, although it is, of course, affected by them. Individuals vary widely in the amount of attention that they devote to their body, but except in sleep, unconsciousness and death, they cannot escape its impact. Its importance is like water to fish—easy to overlook but obvious when it is disturbed.

Behind this fundamental aspect of our awareness lies a parallel concept that has shadowed man's development throughout history; of another, more radiant structure, that infuses the physical body but can function beyond it. Different names have been used to describe this concept; "the subtle body," "the energetic body" or "the body of light". Descriptions of human auras assume that this type of energy body is a normal expression of the life force within the individual. Systems of psychic diagnosis examine the quality of vibrations associated with various portions of the subtle body in order to detect imbalances, and to determine which psychic and mental approaches will restore health. But originally,

Fig. 1. The Chakras

interest in the subtle body was as a vehicle for human development. Matters of mental and physical health came later.

THE CHAKRAS

Descriptions of the subtle body vary in detail, complexity and, in some cases, basic design. But the elements involved are universal. These elements are, in their simplest form, energy centers (chakras) and the connections between them.

Each energy center can be described separately as a kind of isolated organ, like the stomach or the liver. The major chakras are typically located at:

a. the base of the spine;
b. the sex organs;
c. the lower belly;
d. the upper chest;
e. the throat;
f. the center of the eyebrows (third eye); and
g. the crown of the head.

The pathways connecting the chakras with each other and with the rest of the physical body can be mapped like a rarified lymphatic system. The temptation is to approach either the separate structures or the complex pathways connecting them as physical phenomena, which they are not. No dissection has ever found a chakra. If they exist, it is on a more subtle realm of energy relations. Artists attempting to express the inherent ambiguities of the subtle body have suggested this intermixing of dimensions by interpenetrating lights and muted structural boundaries.

In reading the literature on this subject one is immediately struck by the detail with which the material is presented. For example, the chakra in the lower belly is traditionally described as follows:

> The Manipura Chakra is governed by the fire element. It looks like a ten petalled-lotus within which is a red triangle with three T-shaped swastika marks. Its seed mantra is "Ram".

On the other hand, there is comparatively little questioning of the basis on which these very specific descriptions rest. This is exceedingly strange because, unlike the physical body, the very existence of the subtle body is subject to question.

Descriptions of the subtle body usually emphasize the different energy centers. Since each of these centers is associated with easily identifiable human functions this orientation is natural. But the more important question of how they interrelate as a system is often underplayed, or simply overlooked.

Thus the heart center is depicted as a source of love and compassion. The "hara" center in the lower belly is identified with the life force, internal balance and effective physical functioning. But these centers, while distinctly different, are not independent of each other. Whatever happens to one center affects all the others, as in any system.

In the physical body the purpose of each physiological system is clear. The digestive system absorbs and breaks down potential nourishment, eliminating what cannot be burned. The circulatory network transports food and waste products into and out of all areas of the body. The nervous system carries messages and coordinates information. All of these interacting functions are delicately balanced and, for the most part, work instinctively.

But what is the analogous purpose of the energetic body? Any answer at this point would be tentative. One useful model views the subtle body as roughly similar to the physical digestive system. But unlike the digestive system, it cannot act instinctively. If it could, everyone would have a functioning subtle body which, most teachings agree, requires a great deal of time and effort.

Fig. 2. The Subtle body is experienced through sensation.

Perhaps the biggest stumbling block to the understanding of the subtle body is that it doesn't exist in the ordinary sense. You cannot touch it or weigh it. Does this mean that it is a universal fantasy, recurring in various cultures, interesting in its symbolic content but not connected to any enduring reality? The symbolic content is certainly there. But the subtle body can be experienced in the same way as the physical body; through sensation.

Try an experiment. Shake your hands out as if there were a liquid on them that you wanted to cast off. Next, slowly bring them together, palms facing each other. Notice the moment when they seem to impinge on each other's energy field. This may be experienced as a sudden rise in temperature in both hands. If you feel it, experiment with moving your hands slowly apart and then together again, until you convince yourself of the reality of the sensation. Then hold your hands precisely at the place where the sensation first becomes evident to you. Allow the energy to build. After this happens, see if you can slowly move your hands apart without losing the sensation. Did anything happen, or not? If it did, how do you interpret it? Just because you felt a sensation in your hands does not prove that the energetic body exists. But it does support the possibility.

The teachers of subtle body practices usually suggest that if you follow their teachings, you will gradually experience an inner unfolding of the subtle body that is felt as an immediate sensation. Perhaps these experiences may be accompanied by mystical visions or psychic experiences, but that is secondary. What is crucial is that the immediate sensations corresponding to the location and function of energy centers is subject to verification by the individual, if he will follow directions and make certain efforts over time. Belief is not required. An experimental attitude is all that is necessary.

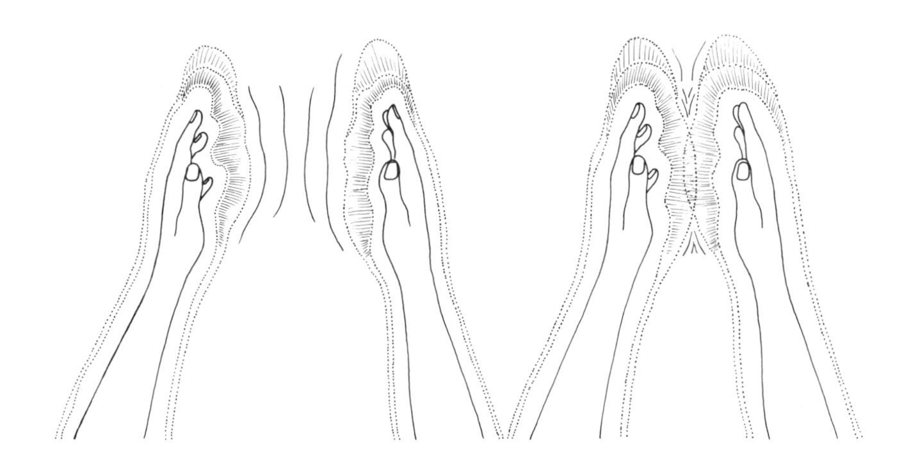

Fig. 3. Sensing the energy between the palms

While the preceding approach seems simple, the actual state of the literature on the subtle body is confusing. Consider the following examples:

In the Hindu tradition, the navel (lower belly) center is associated with fire, the color red, and the syllable "Ram." In Tibetan Buddhism the navel center is associated with water, the color white, and the syllable "Vam." It is hard to see how both versions could be true.

Furthermore, color symbolism in different chakra systems is contradictory. For example, in his book *Energy Ecstacy*[1] Bernard Gunther, relying principally on the Hindu tradition, gives the chakra colors, going from bottom to top as: red-orange, kelly green, yellow gold, sky blue and indigo-purple. In the Buddhist system they are, in the same order: yellow, white, red, green and blue. In color therapy and New Age symbolism they are different from either of the foregoing and also from each other. If one takes these descriptions as objective psychic experiences, then these differences are likely to puzzle the reader since, whatever may have been intended, the traditions involved present these color connections as if they were objective.

Finally, to further compound the confusion, some energy body systems describe the chakras as located along the front of the body, some inside the spine, and others along the center line of the body. Since each system is quite precise about these locations, the innocent reader seeking guidance and clarity has a right to be puzzled by these apparent contradictions.

One of the underlying purposes of this book is to resolve some of these differences by separating the superficial and arbitrary distinctions from the underlying essential ones. All systems, for example, identify specific energy centers and their interconnections. They are typically related to specific sounds, colors, and various other forms of symbolism such as animals and divinities. Even though the symbolism varies, the types of symbols do not.

In regard to the role played by the subtle body within the broader scheme of human spiritual evolution, some traditions view it as central, whereas in others it may appear almost incidental. As an example of the latter, Zen Buddhism places major emphasis on the breakdown of logical functioning so that a higher form of understanding becomes possible. However, further examination reveals that great importance is placed on the navel chakra as the major center of human awareness. Furthermore, it is often believed that utilizing this center as the focus of concentration will eventually activate the energy body in a more complete form.

Regardless of its relative visibility, it should become increasingly clear as we sift through the accumulated wisdom and debris of the ages that the energetic body constitutes a vital link in the attainment of higher inner development. It is a system for creating higher energies through a form of inner alchemy. Since any kind of organic growth requires the proper food, the subtle body, which is capable of generating this nourishment, is essential for any fundamental inner transformation to occur.

Even today, when information on chakras and auras is more widespread, and to some extent taken for granted, it is incredible to think that a mechanism vital for our inner development exists in latent form within each individual, and that it is virtually unknown by a broad range of the population.

One of the basic purposes of this book is to introduce the reader to simple methods by which the reality of this statement can be tested. To have this opportunity is vital not only as a means of intellectually assimilating the material, but also for coming to an organic understanding of what is involved. Our underlying purpose is not scholarly. We are basically concerned with helping readers to apply what they learn to further their own inner development.

An example of one such method is the following:

Place your attention about an inch above where your eyebrows converge. Keep your attention on this spot in a relaxed manner. When you have a clear sensation at that point, allow your awareness to penetrate a little below the surface of the skin. After you feel that happen, say to yourself, "This is the center of my experience." Then, whatever else occurs, keep part of your awareness on this spot for 60 seconds. If you wish, take the forefinger of your right hand and slowly lift it until you make gentle contact with that spot on your forehead. After 10 seconds remove your finger and notice the effect.

If something seems to have occurred, you might wish to take a further step. Keeping your awareness focused on the spot in your forehead, notice your breathing. It has been going on all the time without you paying attention to it. If you keep your awareness in the center of your lower forehead as you breathe in, you will tend to draw extra energy to that place. If you hold your breath briefly and relax, it will give the energy that you have brought there a chance to expand. Then, when you let go and breathe out, you will have the chance to surrender any physical or emotional tension that you are holding in the forehead. Try coordinating your awareness and your breathing in this manner

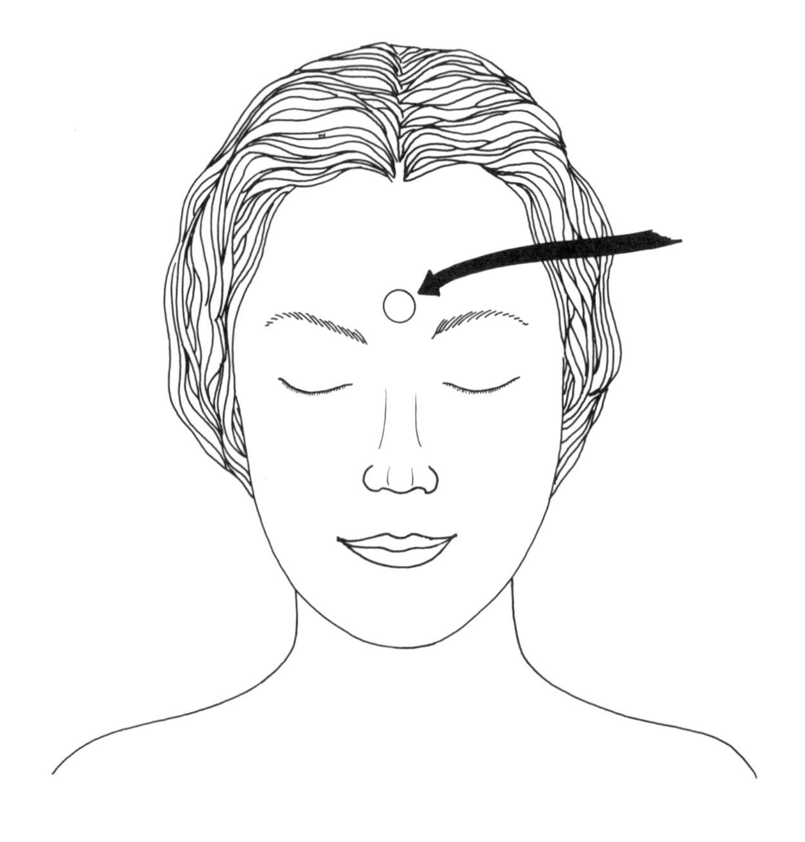

Fig. 4. Place your attention slightly above where your eyebrows converge.

for a few minutes. After this experiment you may have your first taste of what it is like to begin consciously to open a chakra; in this case the third eye.

OPENING CHAKRAS

While it is generally assumed in working with the energetic body that it is a conscious experience to be developed through the proper inner exercises, it is also true that spontaneous experiences involving the opening of the chakras do occur. The main value of such experiences is that they demonstrate to the person involved that the center is actually there, whether or not they have ever heard of it, or would have believed in it if they had.

Perhaps the center that is most likely to open spontaneously is the heart chakra. Think of a time when you were with someone you loved, under very relaxed conditions, in front of a fire or sharing a quiet meal. Whatever the circumstances, one of the sensations you may have noticed was a warm, radiant expanding feeling in the center of your upper chest. If you can remember something of this nature, you have experienced an opening of your heart chakra.

Another type of opening that may have occurred involves the center in the lower belly. Most people have at one time or another experienced a sense of effortless coordination while engaged in a physical activity. It may have been during an athletic event, hiking, or dancing. Whatever the setting, such moments are associated with a heightened sense of awareness, greater relaxation in the midst of activity, a sensation of being lighter, and a feeling that the physical actions occur without much conscious effort on our part. If that experience is at all familiar to you, the chakra in your lower belly was probably open and functioning.

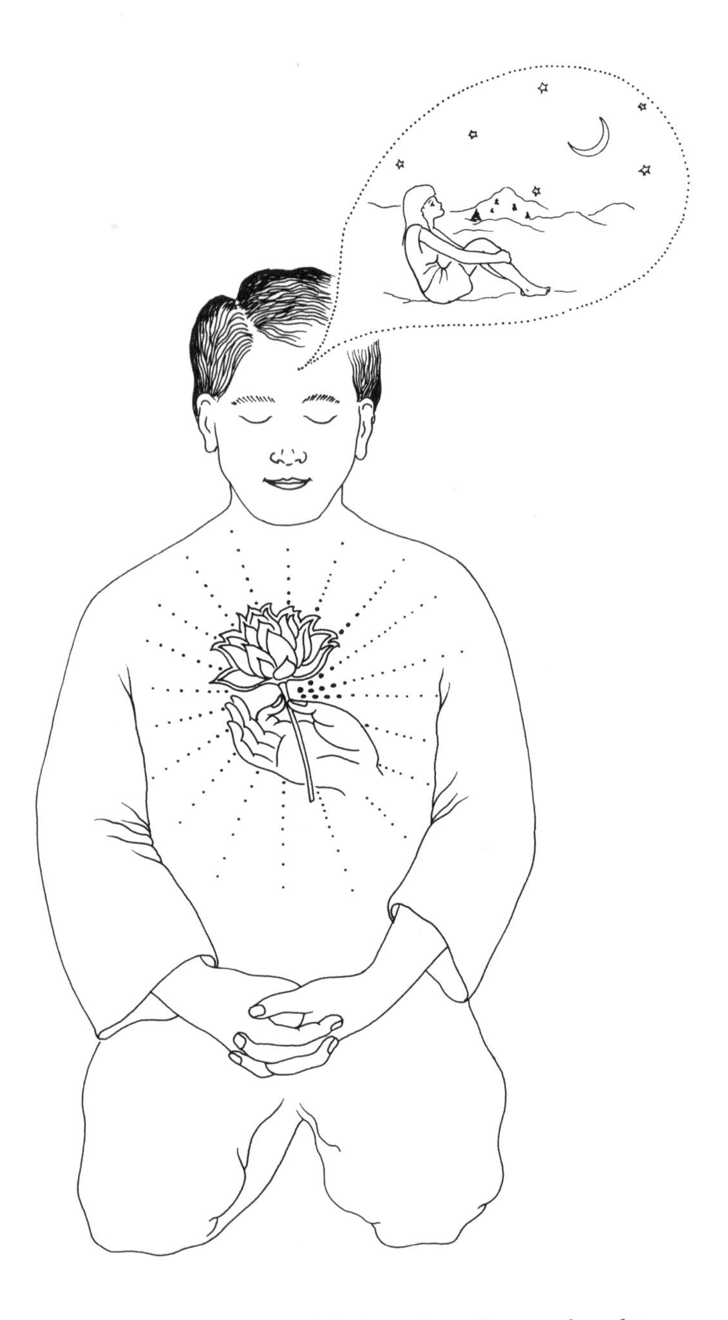

Fig. 5. The spontaneous opening of the heart by a pleasant thought.

Perhaps the most familiar experience for most people is of the inner flow that occurs in a relaxed and harmonious body. This flow can take various directions, some of which do, and some of which do not correspond to traditional pathways in the subtle body. Think of a time when you were free from worry and responsibility, perhaps camping in the wilderness or on the seashore close to nature. Under such conditions you may have felt a great surge of well-being and relaxation and noticed a kaleidoscope of shifting sensations that flowed naturally and effortlessly into each other, creating their own balance and adjustment. At that moment nothing else is necessary. You are content!

While it is natural to focus on the opening of separate energy centers, their interconnections are equally important. Different traditions vary considerably in their emphasis on these interconnections or in their recognition of them. In Kundalini Yoga the major channel for these connections is along the spine, with two subsidiary pathways that twist around in a kind of double helix. In Buddhism the two subsidiary channels are straight. In Taoism a veritable landscape of energy circuits is described in detail. These differences are not necessarily contradictory, but may be due to focusing on different practices or on different levels of practice. In addition, over time, elements of these teachings may have been forgotten. Given the magnitude of the time scales involved (some over thousands of years), it is remarkable how much has been retained.

An energy center is very much like a flower bud. If it is properly cared for and receives the necessary sunshine, the bud opens and turns into a flower. The interconnections between the centers are more like a subtle circulation system. They can develop leaks, holes, or become clogged up with garbage and debris. In working with these interconnections, one must become a spiritual electrician or a psychic plumber, in order to repair the connections and balance the flow between centers.

There is a whole array of methods to help clear the psychic system. Some are strange and complex, others are quite simple. Consider the following:

Sit comfortably. Let your open hands hang down at your sides. Ask in a voice that seems to come from your heart center, "Please help me to surrender my negative psychic tensions." Then relax and see what happens. If the exercise takes, you will feel a warmth and tingling in your hands as the negative psychic tension begins to flow out of them. If you feel nothing, ask again with greater sincerity. Listen to your own voice as you ask, and see if

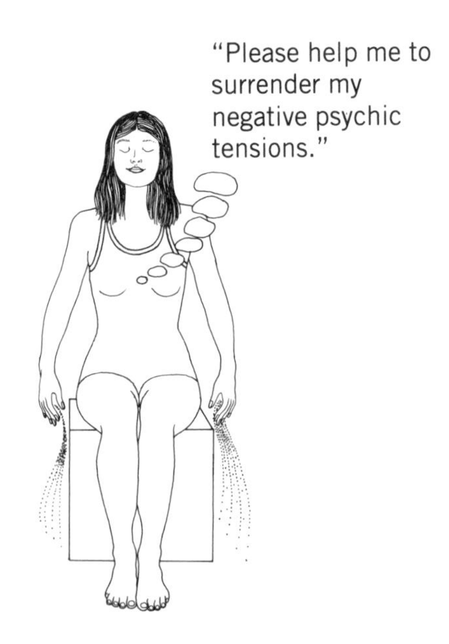

Fig. 6. Surrendering negativity

you believe that it is sincere. After the process has gone on for a few minutes shake your hands, make a fist, and the flow will stop.

AN HOLISTIC VIEW

Over the course of time some traditions have emphasized working more with specific chakras and less with their interconnections. This is unfortunate. If the various channels cannot communicate, they will not be able to fulfill their underlying purpose. The chakras and the network that encloses them are part of a whole that cannot be understood, and cannot function properly, outside the context of the system that constitutes their frame of reference. This holistic orientation is often portrayed by showing sacred individuals and divinities with auras around their bodies and haloes surrounding their heads. If this type of symbolism occurred in only one or two traditions, it could be viewed as coincidental. But it is too pervasive to be an accident. A simpler explanation is that holy persons become that way precisely because a higher level of cosmic energy flows through them. It is this experience that religious art seeks to reproduce, utilizing a combination of psychic sight and traditional representation.

Students of the human energy field attest to the fact that all people have auras—colored emanations that are radiated as part of the life process of the individual. The frequency and intensity of the colors symbolize the level of energy transformation that is occurring. Dark brown is less desirable than shining orange. A person in whom the subtle body is fully functioning has greatly accelerated the transformation process within him. This is expressed as an expanded and purified energy field around the physical body. It is no accident that the aura of holy people is drawn in gold, which is rare, pure and radiant.

Sacred pictures may leave one with the impression that the particular saint was born with a halo or attained it in a moment of great illumination. This is misleading. The light that is shown was created as the overflow of a gradual process of development, in much the same way that the size of a tree trunk expresses a continuous growth process over many seasons. Religious artists have been telling us throughout history that the subtle body exists, and that the truest expression of the sacred in human experience is the quality of light radiated by the individual.

According to a number of mystical systems, the subtle body is one of a series of progressively more refined human manifestations. Although the terminology varies and the cross-comparisons are sometimes confusing, the recurrence of these conceptions suggests a more universal model of spiritual development. In Mahayana Buddhism the Buddha is viewed as having three bodies: "Nirmanakaya" (body of transformation), "Sambhogakaya" (body of enjoyment) and "Dharmakaya" (body of reality). In Hinduism the gross, subtle, and causal bodies offer a partial correspondence. The crucial consideration in the present context is that in order to get to the higher bodies, and the level of awareness and function that they incorporate, you must activate and utilize the energy body. In this sense it constitutes a crucial intervening link in the inner development of the individual.

In many systems the importance of the energy body is underplayed. Others seem to totally ignore it. In religions and mystical paths emphasizing love, whether Christian, Moslem or Hindu, the approach seems completely focused on devotion accompanied by obedience. One can interpret this approach as cultivating the heart chakra, but if this is being done, it is certainly an indirect approach.

Other ways emphasize mind control. Examples of this orientation are found in the Kabbala, Raja Yoga, Zen Buddhism, and various tantric visualization practices. These systems focus on efforts to control, guide, or eliminate thoughts. Here again, these methods may relate indirectly to opening the chakras in the head, but little or no mention is made of them.

Often a little creative detective work reveals aspects of subtle body functioning in approaches that have nothing direct to say about them. Several modern examples can be given. The late

Fig. 7. The nimbus in Christ

Hindu teacher J. Krishnamurti went to great lengths to avoid most traditional approaches and rejected most familiar teachers and teachings. His major emphasis was on cultivating awareness outside the context of any tradition. He did not acknowledge the subtle body. Nevertheless, it is interesting to read in his own diary[2] of a period of intense and painful energy flow in his head

Fig. 8. The aura in a Buddhist diety

and spine going on intermittently for 40 years as the accompaniment of various spiritual experiences. This description is quite similar to accounts of the arousal of kundalini, which is certainly a vital aspect of subtle body practices.

Another example is the Hindu saint Sri Ramana Maharishi, who focused on the question "Who am I?" as the most direct path to enlightenment. In explaining the values of his system a major disciple, Sri Sadhu Om[3] has recently explained that the "I" on awakening in the morning shoots from the heart center to the brain, and from there through the various energy channels which distribute the sense of identity throughout the body. In this description the chakra system is being recognized, even though it is generally underplayed or ignored in the Maharishi's method in order to emphasize the importance of one's identity as the major point of concentration.

One way to interpret the preceding is to conclude that the individual is influenced by the tradition within which he has been nourished and will interpret his experiences in that light. If part of that background includes a system incorporating the subtle body concept, then his experiences will find ways to support it. If the emphasis is on sudden transformation and revelation, it may be minimized. But if the subtle body is real, and the experiences of the individual are also real, then the two must relate, even if one must search to find the connection.

In the succeeding chapters of Part I, various models of the subtle body are described, analyzed, and compared. Some of the material may strike the reader as strange or even dubious. But the crucial question is always whether it can be experienced. If it can, then its importance is potentially very great. If not, the most elaborate conceptions will evaporate like mist and need not concern us further.

CHAPTER TWO

The Hindu Tradition

The origins of the Hindu tradition are hard to trace, but the high points of its history are relatively easy to identify. Starting about 3,500 years ago when the Aryans invaded Northern India, a new wave of influence was imposed upon the indigenous Dravidian culture, which had previously worshipped the earth and the feminine as the embodiment of creative energy. The Aryan influence, in contrast, was masculine and deified the sun. The two cultures were directly contradictory. But Hindus have specialized over the years in absorbing almost any influence and, in the process, creating a unique cultural synthesis, particularly in relation to philosophical and spiritual matters.

The major literary achievements of early Indian society, such as the Vedas—including the Samhitas and Brahmanas (of which the Upanishads are the most famous), the Sutras, and such classical epics as the Ramayana and the Mahabharata—stand on their own merits even today. But however high their literary and philosophical content may be, they have little to say about the subtle body. There are, however, interesting exceptions. For example in the Chandogya Upanishad it is said:

> One hundred & one are the channels of the heart.
> Of these but one extend right up to the head;
> Ascend thereby to immortality!

The rest, at thy departing,
Everywhere get lost.[1]

This account refers directly to the connection between the heart and crown chakras, both major centers in the subtle body. These centers are presented as if the reader was already quite aware of the context in which they were introduced. As with all Indian literature, dates and contexts are hard to establish because they arose from an oral tradition carried by folk singers and teachers earlier than any time that we can identify.

In any case, these complex strands did not come into a fully integrated expression until the Gupta period, about the seventh and eighth century A.D. This is reflected in the art of the time, and is expressed most completely in the Tantric tradition, which took as its central theme precisely the total integration of all cultural elements in one comprehensive transformative expression.

The tantric scriptures themselves are endlessly varied, covering such matters as medicine, magic, astrology, science, government, interpersonal relations and, finally, the subtle body. The latter topic was usually handled under the heading of "tantric yoga."

THE NATURE OF YOGA

Yoga is essentially a practical science of inner evolution based upon the cumulative experience of students and teachers who have devoted a major part of their lives to its practice. There are many forms of yoga, each created to suit a different type of individual. One means of classifying them employed by W. Y. Evans-Wentz[2] is as follows:

1. Hatha - physical control
2. Laya - mind control
   a. Bhakti - love

b. Shakti - creative energy
c. Mantra - sacred sounds
d. Yantra - sacred forms
3. Dhyana - thought
4. Raja - discrimination
a. Jnana - knowledge
b. Karma - activity
c. Kundalini - psychic nerve force
d. Samadhi - ecstatic self-knowledge

The various types of yogas can also be grouped as introductory, intermediate and advanced. In general, Hatha Yoga is viewed as preliminary to other forms of practice, while Raja and Kundalini Yoga are considered to be the highest forms.

Swami Rama, founder of the Himalayan International Institute, identifies Kundalini Yoga as the crown of yogic experience in the following terms: "Among all the approaches to studying the internal realm the science of kundalini yoga is the most advanced."[3]

This emphasis by a highly respected modern authority is of considerable importance in the present context, because kundalini yoga is based upon and utilizes the subtle body.

Fig. 9. Yogi representation in ancient Indus Valley seal

The practices of yoga are considerably older than any written scripture referring to them. There is a very early statue of what appears to be an archetypal yogi that was found in Mohenjo-Daro and has been dated at about 2400 B.C. But whatever the origin of yoga in a generic sense, it is the tantric tradition of the seventh to tenth centuries A.D. that is our immediate focus. It permeates Hinduism, Buddhism and Jainism as a counterpoint to the more orthodox forms of these religions, all of which share as a traditional part of their philosophy the rejecting of worldly experience as a method for discovering inner reality.

TANTRIC YOGA

The tantric practitioner, in contrast, believes that the senses can be used to achieve ecstatic enlightenment. The senses are not to be denied but transformed, so that instead of leading the individual ever deeper into the spider web of the world, they can help him retrace his way back to the source.

This fundamental difference in outlook leads the tantric to employ methods and to take actions that diverge from many traditional religious practices. He may meditate among corpses, engage in orgiastic rituals or perform magical ceremonies designed to attract the presence of a Deity.

The average person might view these actions as primitive, bizarre or sacrilegious if he observed them. But it is impossible to judge their intent from the outside. For each visible action there is a corresponding inner condition that must be met, and which is inherently invisible. But whatever the content of a particular ritual might be, however formal or spontaneous, it is designed to foster the joyous expression of energy which the tantric absorbs as it is liberated to further his own growth.

Inner development of any kind involves moving against resistance and making efforts that lead toward a particular goal. The tantric uses every form of sensualism to generate motivation toward the goal instead of treating these sources of attraction as obstacles. He says "yes" to the world and proceeds to recreate it to help him achieve his own development.

This viewpoint has much in common with that of the creative artist. Painters, sculptors and playwrights each take the elements

Fig. 10. An Aghori Tantric meditating on the corpse of a young woman

of everyday life and transform them into an expression of a higher order. As individuals they may be one-sided, but in their art they achieve a resolution of their experience that aims to bring them aesthetic fulfillment.

The tantric is not interested in producing an external product—the object of his creativity is himself. Toward this end he approaches almost any facet of his life as a potential ritual that can be utilized as a means for reaching a higher level of inner development.

Tantric practices employ a variety of sensual modalities to achieve this end; sight, sound, touch and taste all woven together to create a ritual action in a particular setting. The most elaborate artistic expression of tantric practice is visual. Perhaps the most famous form is the mandala; a cosmic diagram designed to alter the state of consciousness of the person viewing it. Many mandalas are quite beautiful, but that is secondary. Their primary purpose is to act as a gateway to higher dimensions of consciousness. All tantric art is designed for use, not for decoration. This does not mean that it cannot be gorgeous, barbaric, or serene. But its objective is always to bring the viewer to a higher level of experience, not to portray everyday reality as an end in itself.

The tantric orientation focuses on energy rather than on structure. It continually emphasizes the identification of the energy flow that lies behind visible appearances. Since the Hindu goddess Kundalini is the universal creative power, the tantric tradition is a natural context for subtle body work as formulated in kundalini yoga.

Tantric yoga developed in a caste society in which each member was born to occupy an unchangeable position that he could not expect to alter during his lifetime. Intermarriage between castes was forbidden. Endless rules governed every aspect of daily life. The Hindu tantric made a conscious attempt to destroy,

Fig. 11. Mandala of the five Buddha families

or at least to suspend, all of these prohibitions as a means of liberating the energy that they constrained. Thus, in the famous Chakra Ceremony, social, marital, sexual, dietary and caste rules were all systematically violated. The effect must have been far more powerful than we, as members of a free society, can imagine.

The stereotype of the tantric tradition is that it involves exotic sexual practices. While there is some basis for this idea, it is like believing that the essence of Western culture is the hot dog—it is only one element. Nevertheless, the tantrics did succeed in overcoming the effect of the Aryan masculine impact on Indian society and brought sexual influences back into balance by emphasizing the importance of the feminine principle. The central image of tantric philosophy is the balance of masculine and feminine as the basis of higher consciousness. This view is at odds with traditional religious sentiment, which often represses sexuality and may require that the aspirant surrender all worldly pleasures as a means of obtaining enlightenment. While the goals of each are essentially the same—attaining a cosmic state of being—the approach is totally different. It is no accident that the emphasis on the subtle body's energetic development finds a congenial environment in the tantric tradition.

Kundalini Yoga was originally described in a variety of tantric texts that were summarized in the Satcakranirupana during the middle of the 16th century. In modern times the subject was made available to the west in *The Serpent Power*[4]. This book is devoted to a detailed exposition of the anatomy of the subtle body within the context of a cosmology that viewed the world as the play of creative energy.

THE ANATOMY OF THE SUBTLE BODY

Before examining the specific descriptions of the chakras in The Serpent Power, it may be helpful to clarify some of the implicit and explicit assumptions that seem to underlie its basic orientation.

The first is that the subtle body is part of the universal inheritance of a human being. It is not the creation of any particular culture or tradition. Furthermore, in the Hindu view, it already exists. What must be done is to uncover it and help it to function.

Second, the subtle body is made up of energy centers or

chakras, the channels between them, and the channels from them to all parts of the physical body. These channels are called *nadi*. Neither the chakras nor the nadis are visible on the physical level, but they can be experienced through psychic vision and physical sensation. On the whole, Hindu texts place much greater emphasis on the nature of the chakras than on the connections between them, although both are recognized.

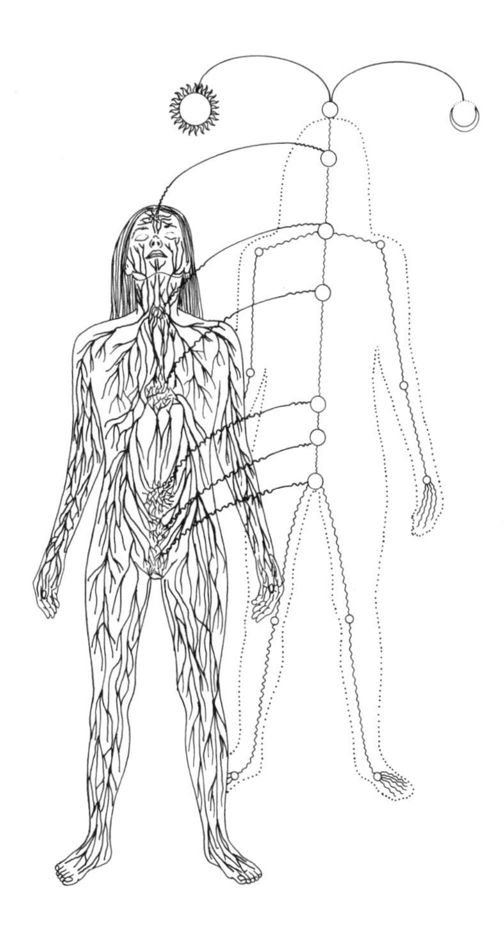

Fig. 12. The physical body is connected with the subtle body through the "nadis".

Fig. 13. The three bodies

Third, the subtle body is part of a system of higher bodies. While various Hindu philosophies describe different numbers of such bodies, the simplest version contains three: physical, subtle and cosmic. The physical body is studied by physiology and medicine. The subtle body is the subject of this book. The cosmic body is the means by which the individual relates to the universe as a total experience. While it is not always explicitly stated it is generally assumed that the sequence is cumulative, starting from the physical, moving to the subtle, and reaching its highest expression in the cosmic. The contrast between the subtle and cosmic bodies can be clearly seen from typical drawings of each. The significance of the particular symbolism may not be clear, but the difference in the dimensionality of what is being portrayed is quite evident.

It is hard for a westerner to begin to comprehend the endless scriptural distinctions that exist in Hindu religious literature. Any conclusion that might be drawn about the subtle body is extended, contradicted or altered by some other authority, in an endless array of interpretations and reinterpretations of the classical texts.

An examination of such scriptures as the Satcakranirupana and a variety of more ancient texts on which it is based, such as the Matrekabhedatantra, Tararahasya, Saradatilaka and at least 13 additional texts, yields a model with general agreement among all these authorities, one that is surprisingly simple in its basic design. While there are varying numbers of chakras recognized in different tantras and scripture, the most universally described are:

a. Muladhara
b. Svadhisthana
c. Manipura
d. Anahata
e. Visuddha
f. Ajna
g. Sahasrara.

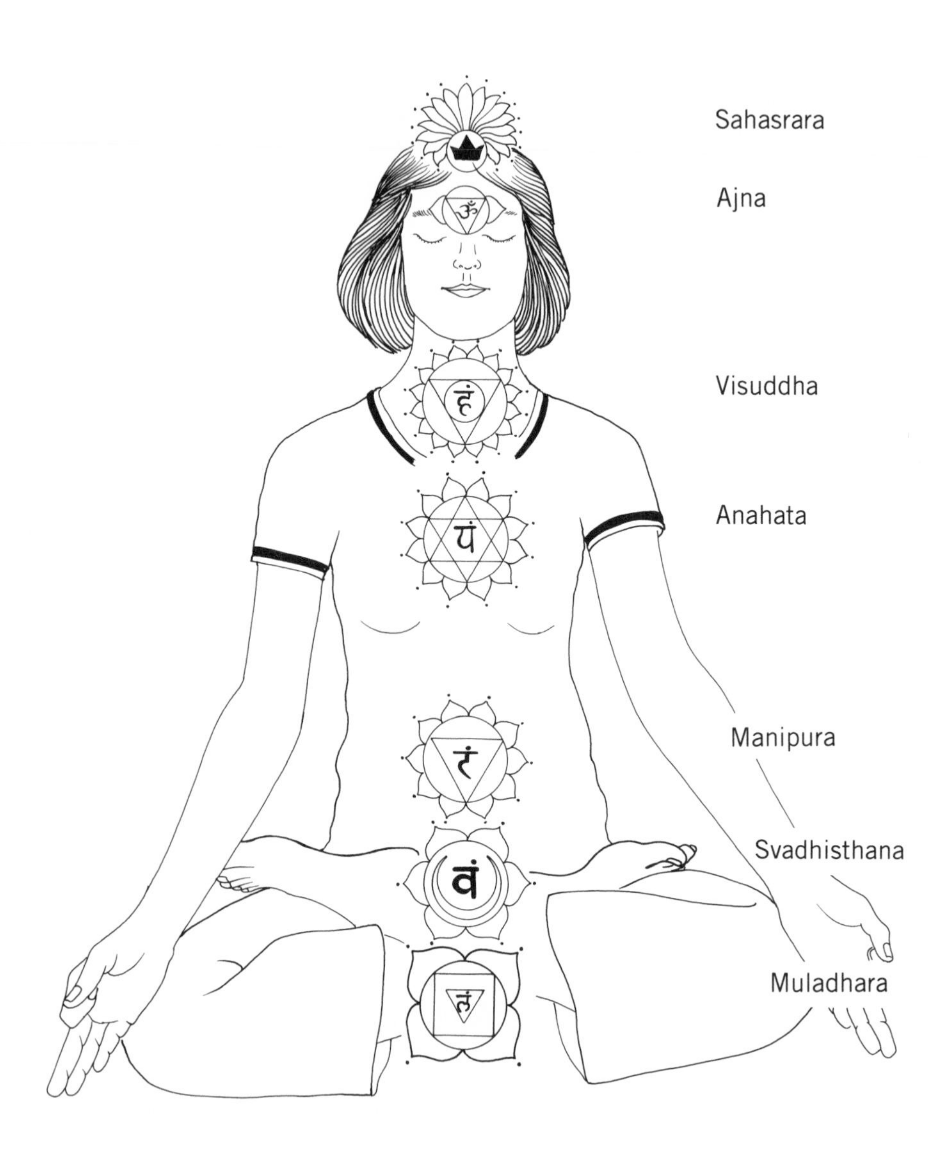

Fig. 14. The seven chakras

Figure 14 shows where these chakras are located in the human organism.

This is the classic Hindu view of the organization of the subtle body with the chakras strung from the base of the spine upward along its axis, culminating in the crown of the head.

In order to clarify the relation of the chakras to the subtle anatomy of the spine a further diagram is necessary.

In figure 15 the spine is shown as a series of sheaths. Not all authorities agree about what takes place within the various sheaths. For example, some scriptures state that the Ida and Pingala and the Sushumna are outside all the sheaths, whereas most others place them within. But the preponderance of opinion is summarized in figure 15. The six lower chakras are located in the channel within the Citrini, which is also the channel through which the kundalini flows. In the very center of all the sheaths (sometimes called the Brahma Nadi) is a sacred space where five deities reside; Brahma, Visnu, Rudra, Sadasiva and Isvara.

The chakras are related to each other and the physical body by a series of energy pathways of decreasing size, much like the blood vessels in the circulation system. It is said that there are 72,000 such pathways. Whether or not this numerical precision is misleading, it is clear that there are a vast number of them.

THE DESCRIPTION OF THE CHAKRAS

A study of the various relevant scriptures and tantras that are summarized in *The Serpent Power* suggests a high level of complexity in the description of the chakras themselves covering such variables as: locations in the body; seed mantras; yantras (sacred diagrams and shapes); associated deities, both masculine and feminine; vehicles; qualities; spheres; linga; yoni; elements; forms;

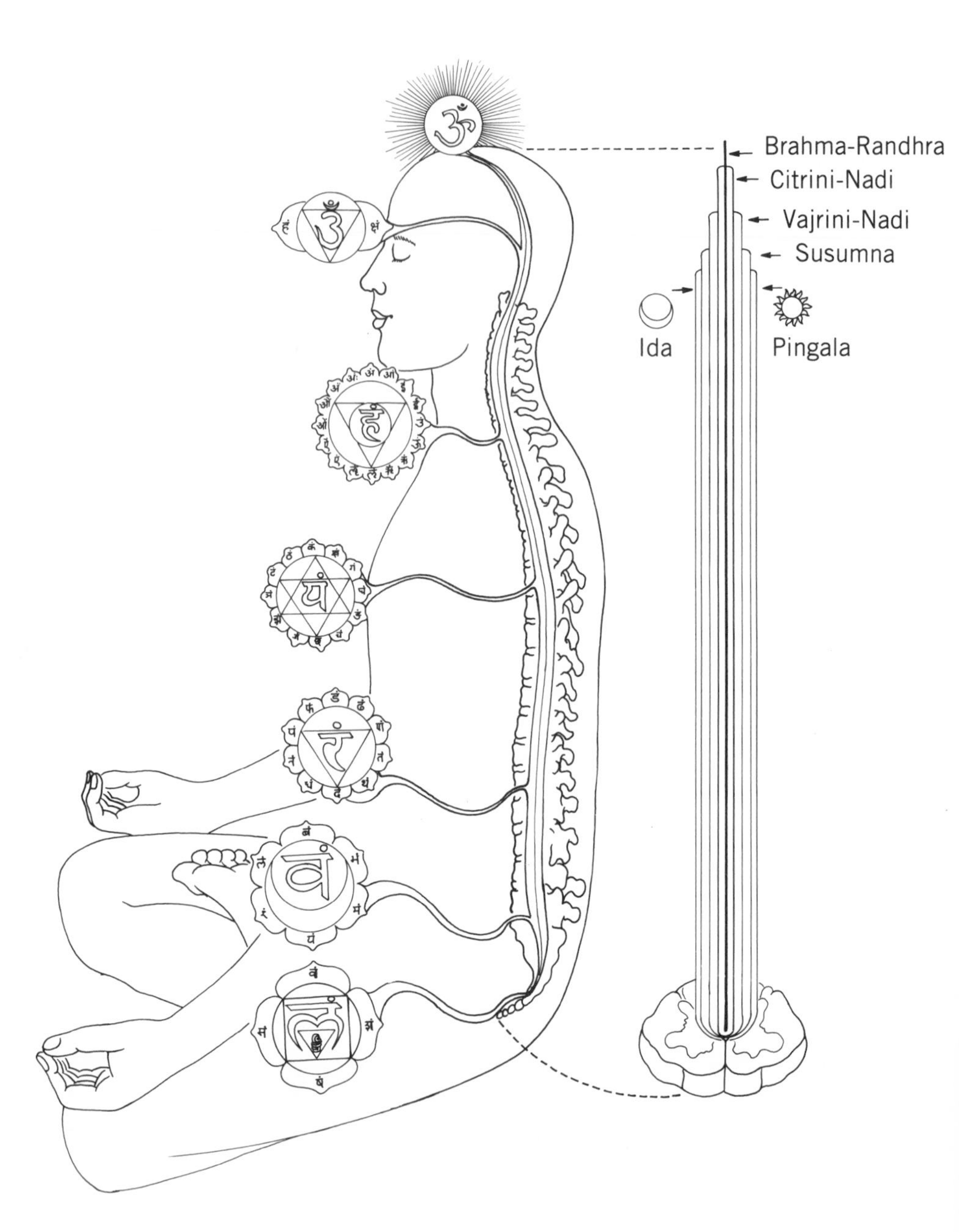

Fig. 15. The spinal sheaths in crossection

associated senses; and the effects on the practitioner who focuses on them.

For, example, the base chakra is described as follows:

> It is located above the anus and below the genitals at the base of the spine. It has four crimson petals on which the golden letters VA, SA, SA and SA are inscribed. Inside the petals is a square symbolizing the earth element surrounded by 8 shining spears. The seed mantra of the earth element LAM is within the square. Brahma dwells in the lap of the seed mantra. He has four faces and four arms and is seated on a swan. Indra, the king of the immortals, is also in this area. He sits on the king of the elephants, Airavata. He is yellow and holds thunderbolts in his hands. Dakini is the presiding feminine deity. She has brilliant red eyes and four shining arms. Her hands hold a spear, a staff piercing a human skull, a sword and a goblet filled with

Fig. 16. The base chakra

> ambrosia. She has fangs that show her fierce temper. She gives to yogis knowledge of the elements, but scares animals and ordinary people. In the center of the square is a triangle called Tripura in which resides the Lord of Life. There is a linga around which the sleeping Kundalini is coiled three and a half times. Kundalini is like a million moons. She has four arms and three eyes. Her hands hold a book, a lute, and make the gesture of granting boons and dispelling fear. As she awakens she is seated on a lion and appears to continuously change shape. Meditating on the goddess enables the yogi to become healthy, happy, learned, a powerful speaker, and a lord of men.

Each of the other chakras is described in equal detail. Any effort to summarize this information in tabular form is bound to lose a good deal of the symbolic detail, which is of importance in the complete analysis of the chakra itself.

For example, if we select the category "presiding deity" in the Anahata Chakra, this deity would be described as seated on a red lotus. She has three eyes and four arms that hold a skull, a noose and are expressing mudras for the elimination of anxiety and fear. Her body is brilliant; her heart is softened by drinking nectar. She is dressed in yellow and wears jewels and bone garlands. Within a tabular form she would simply be described as "Kakini". The rest of the information would be lost, although it could be regained by consulting the original sources if the necessity arose. For purposes of comparative analysis, however, a tabular approach is essential. In table 1 a considerable amount of information is summarized, even though a great deal more is eliminated in the process.

IMPLICATIONS

There are several basic issues raised by the Hindu conception of the subtle body. First, what is the meaning of the symbolic complexity of the description of the chakras? Is it real, in an everyday sense, or is it more in the nature of a dream state experience?

Second, how does the subtle body connect with the lower and higher bodies of the individual, and in what sense do all these bodies exist? It is clear that the subtle or energy body is intermediate, but it is not evident how it got there or precisely what its importance may be. Kundalini Yoga is considered one of the highest, or the highest, yoga. But why? Is it because the areas of experience contained in the chakras represent the inner aspect of a mystical journey? Certainly the refined symbolism of the chakras emphasizes their different domains.

Why is it so important to open the chakras and activate the subtle body? This is not really made clear in the Hindu literature, except in the general context of growth and development. If the cosmic body exists already and only needs to be contacted, why bother with the subtle body which is, at best, an intermediary? This is the point of view of various sudden enlightenment schools of Hinduism and Buddhism. But just as it is difficult to develop the subtle body if the physical body is diseased or disturbed, it seems reasonable to assume that the cosmic body depends on the subtle body to support it in a similar manner.

Third, to what extent is the tantric orientation related to Kundalini Yoga? Does the openness of the former provide a particularly congenial atmosphere for the pursuit of the latter? And, if so, what does this suggest for those who follow more traditional religious orientations?

The subtle body is essentially a vehicle for the transformation of energy. In the Hindu view the crucial basis of its functioning is the activation of the base chakra, in which the creative goddess Kundalini lies asleep. Much of the technique of Kundalini Yoga,

TABLE 1
The Chakras

	Muladhara Chakra	Svadhisthana Chakra	Manipura Chakra
Location	Base of Spine	Root of genitals	Root of navel
Petal Number, Color & Letters	4 blood red petals with gold letters VA, 'SA, SA, SA	6 vermillion petals with lightning-like letters VA, BHA, MA, YA, RA, LA	10 grey rain cloud-colored petals with blue letters DAM, DHAM, NAM, TAM, THAM, DAM, DHAM, NAM, PAM, PHAM
Bija	LAM	VAM	RAM
Yantra (Form)	Yellow Square	White Crescent	Agni Mandala
Number of Rays and Element	56, Earth	52, Water	62, Fire
Sense or Type of Awareness	Odor	Taste	Sight
Animal	Elephant king with 7 trunks and black collar	Makara, mythic crocodile fish that eats everything	Ram
Diety	(Child) Brahma	Hari Vishnu	Rudra (Vishu)
Sakti	Dakini	Rakini	Lakini (Laksmi)
Effect	Freedom from disease and fear. Mastery of learning and power of speech. Spirit filled with great gladness.	Freedom from the enemies—lust, anger, greed & sloth.	Health and vigor, creativity.

TABLE 1 (cont.)
The Chakras

Anahata Chakra	Visuddha Chakra	Ajna Chakra	Sahasrara Chakra
Heart level	Throat	Above center of eyebrows	Crown of the head
12 crimson petals with vermillion letters KAM, KHAM, GAM, GHAM, NAM, CAM, CHAM, JAM, JHAM, NAM, TAM, THAM	16 smoky purple petals with crimson letters (vowels) A, A, I, I, U, U, R, R, L, L, E, AI, O AU, AM, AH	2 white petals with white letters KSAM, HAM	1,000 petals with the light of 1,000 suns
YAM	HAM	OM	Beyond sound; including all sound
Satknoa, interlocking triangles, 6-pointed star	Circle	Circle with golden inverted triangle, crescent & bindu	Beyond form, Mahabindu of the void
54, Air	72, Space	64, Mind	Total luminosity, Nityananda
Touch	Hearing	Consciousness	Liberation
Black antelope	Snow white 7-trunk elephant	none	none
Isa	Sadasiva	ParamaSiva (Sambhu)	Brahman or, depending on sects, the union Shiva/Shakti, Purusha/Prakriti, Hari-Hara
Kakini	Gauri	Hakini	Nirvana Sakti
Sense control	Serenity, longevity, equanimity	Uninterrupted bliss, witnesses all as one presence	Freedom from time & space

whether it involves special breathing, physical positions and body locks, mantras, mental exercises or direct energy transmission, has as its primary focus the activation of this chakra. Once this has been accomplished a series of distillations occurs in an alchemical manner. The energy rises from the base of the spine, awakening each chakra in turn in an ascending process in which each chakra releases a higher energy than the previous one. The sequence climaxes in the highest chakra, when the thousand-petalled lotus opens and the feminine force of Kundalini meets the masculine force of Shiva contained in the chakra in a kind of cosmic embrace. When the cycle completes itself in this manner all the warmth leaves the body, with the exception of a spot on the top of the head. To the outside observer the yogi appears almost to have died.

In summary, the Hindu tradition is, in one sense, extraordinarily complex. The subtlety of the interpretations that have developed over the last 3,500 years are remarkable. The investment of energy and emotion in otherworldly pursuits is uniquely Hindu in its quality and character.

At the same time, the Hindu model of the subtle body as a series of chakras strung along the spine is very straightforward. It is true that the detailing of the chakras is impressive in its multidimensional character, and in its acknowledgment of 72,000 energy channels. But the basic picture of a system of seven chakras which one ascends like a musical scale is of striking simplicity, particularly in an ancient culture that gave birth to the overwhelming diversity of the tantric tradition.

CHAPTER THREE

BUDDHIST SYSTEMS

The historic Buddha lived over 2,500 years ago. His teachings gave rise to a reform movement within Hinduism. The conditions of the times were somewhat similar to those that gave birth to Christianity. There was great unrest. People were seeking guidance and many new teachers and teachings appeared. In retrospect, the significance of both Buddhism and Christianity is obvious, but at the time it might have been difficult to differentiate them from the many cults that were then flourishing, each promising salvation and enlightenment on its own terms.

After the Buddha's death, Hinayana Buddhism continued to develop as an expression of the work he had left with his followers. Major emphasis during the next 500 years was placed on the individual working out his own enlightenment, either as a hermit who had surrendered the world, or as a member of a strict religious community. Although householders had their place, the more serious followed the lonely path of the Arahat, an enlightened being whose personal attainment might serve as an inspiration to others, but whose success was produced from his own determination and inner efforts.

While Christianity was being founded in the Middle East, Buddhism in India underwent a parallel alteration in the form of Mahayana Buddhism. It is hard to identify this development with a particular date, but one that is often used is the Council of King Kaniska in the first century A.D. In one sense, Mahayana Buddhism undid most of what the historic Buddha had accomplished. His approach had emphasized the elimination of suffering through the surrender of worldly attachments. He ignored all theological questions, did not speak of God, reincarnation, or other favorite topics of Eastern religion and philosophy. His approach was thoroughly practical in its own terms. If a philosophical issue did not help the individual escape his own existential dilemma, he ignored it as irrelevant. He made only one claim for himself; that he had awakened from the dream of the world. Buddhism was not really a religion in the usual sense.

With the coming of Mahayana Buddhism all of this was altered. A whole system of deities, demons and Buddhas, inhabiting a multidimensional universe, was created. The Buddha himself became godlike. Actually, he became greater than the Gods. Endless philosophical and religious elements were introduced. Perhaps most importantly, the concept of the Boddhisattva as the Buddhist ideal was created. The Boddhisattva was a Christ-like figure who surrendered his own enlightenment so that all other beings might be saved.

This broadening of the base of Buddhism greatly extended its popular appeal, since the Hinayana form had been lonely and austere. But it also changed the character of Buddhism in a fundamental way. One wonders what the Buddha would have thought about it, much as one might wonder what Christ would have thought about the churches established in his name. However intriguing such speculations may be, the important point in the present context is that neither form of Buddhism had much to say about the subtle body. Hinayana emphasized codes of conduct and self-observation, to which Mahayana added compassion and a broad array of universal symbols. It is only with the advent of Tantric Buddhism that the subtle body became an explicit element in the Buddhist approach to enlightenment.

There are, however, a few exceptions to this general condition, such as the Tonlin purification, which is a fundamental practice in the Mahayana tradition.[1]

The basic process of Tonlin purification is simple. First you select a particular negative emotion either because you find it in yourself or in the immediate environment. Then you extend your awareness to all others in the world feeling the same emotion.

Fig. 17. The Tonlin purification practice

Then you slowly breathe in, consciously absorbing this negativity into the upper center of the chest where a kind of black hole is located. All the emotion vanishes into this point. You hold your breath to allow the negativity to be transformed. Then as you breathe out, the purified energy is radiated in all directions from a star-like point of light in the same location as the black hole. While it is not clear whether the black and white points are located in the heart center, it is evident that the practice deals with the purification and transformation of energies around and within the practitioner, and to this extent could be classified as a subtle body process, even though it is done primarily for the sake of others.

TANTRIC BUDDHISM

In any case it was only with the coming of Tantric Buddhism that subtle body work became a definite part of Buddhist philosophy and practice. In Tibet, Tantric Buddhism was known as the third vehicle, or Vajrayana Buddhism. It was believed to be the most direct and quickest path to enlightenment, although it was also the most complicated.

Vajrayana Buddhism was developed in India during the same period as Hindu tantra, both coming to maturity in the seventh and eighth centuries A.D. At that time it was foreseen by seers that the tradition would be limited or destroyed in India by future conquerors. A conscious effort was made to transplant the wisdom of the tantras to other, more protected, environments. Of these, Tibet was probably the least accessible and eventually the most successful. While the Himalayan region, including such countries as Nepal, Ladakh, Butan and Sikim, shared these developments in common, it was probably in Tibet that the tantras were cultivated more completely than anywhere else. It was only with the Chinese Communist invasion of Tibet in 1949 that these carefully preserved traditions were virtually forced into the modern world. For the first time, high lamas whom one might have visited only with the greatest difficulty, became relatively accessible, as they made their first trips to the West.

One of the reasons for the extraordinary endurance of an essentially Indian medieval tradition within a Tibetan context was the careful and systematic organization that the material attained over time. Until quite recently, 12 dedicated years of study and practice were required before the student was allowed anywhere near what might be called subtle body work. Whether or not such a lengthy preparation was really necessary may be questioned, but anyone surviving it would certainly place high value on what he was given as a consequence.

While it is true that the subtle body is cultivated in Vajrayana Buddhism, it would be misleading to suggest that its appearance is all that obvious. For example, in John Blofeld's *The Tantric Mysticism of Tibet*[2] the subject does not come up at all, even though such topics as "the essence of the tantric method," "psychic and material symbols," and "general practice and advanced practice" are all covered.

As in Hindu tantra, Vajrayana concerns a vast array of different topics. Even those that are of a strictly mystical character are numerous, including such practices as prostration, guru yoga, generating bodhicitta, regular rituals and special rituals, preparation for death and higher yogas of the formless path such as mahayoga, annuyoga, atiyoga. But the subtle body occurs only under the general heading of "paths of form", including the six yogas of Naropa and a variety of lesser known approaches.

THE SUBTLE BODY IN TANTRIC BUDDHISM

To the casual student it would have appeared until recently that the subtle body, the chakras and the channels were a minor matter in tantric Buddhism. It was only with the recent publication of such works as *Clear Light Of Bliss*[3] that the importance of the subtle body in higher tantric work has become clarified. This book is said by Tibetans to have "spilled the beans" by revealing the heart of advanced yoga practices. The character of the book is suggested by the chapter titles: "Channels, Winds and Drops, Inner Fire, Clear Light and the Four Joys, The Nine Mixings and the Two Seals, Tranquil Abiding, Meditation on Emptiness, The Illusory Body, Clear Light and Union." The first half of the book focusses on the subtle body under the heading "Paths of Form." In the second half the emphasis shifts to the formless path, or what is meant by the "clear light of bliss." The paths of form provide the preparation for the formless paths. Lest there be any doubt, the author, Geshe Kelsang Gyatso states:

> It is through gaining control over the winds, and drops flowing through these channels that the union of simultaneous great bliss and emptiness is achieved.[4]

The channels referred to are the nadis. The winds are the energy flow. The drops are a refined energy produced by alchemical inner work. White drops come from the crown of the head, red drops from the navel where the cauldron of transformation is located.

It is reasonable to conclude that the subtle body is a central concern of tantric Buddhism, although it has been somewhat obscured by the variety of other topics that are covered, perhaps intentionally, so as to leave an essential key in the hands of the Guru. This is quite in keeping with the Tibetan tradition in which vital elements of a scripture are omitted and must be supplied

Fig. 18. The Buddhist three bodies

orally by the teacher. In this way the purity of the oral transmission can be maintained.

Beyond the subtle body itself is a somewhat confusing system of higher bodies. There are several reasons for this confusion. First, there are many different bodies that are described, but what often seems to be meant are states of consciousness rather than levels of materiality. Another source of confusion is that what are often described are Buddha bodies rather than human bodies. Buddha bodies are evolved human bodies. The major ones are the Truth Body, the Complete Enjoyment Body and the Emànation Body. The Truth Body is the embodiment of omnipotent wisdom in emptiness and can be equated with the space body. The Complete Enjoyment Body abides in a higher realm of experience. It can be equated with the refined subtle body. Finally the Emanation Body is the actual physical body of the Buddha, but in his case he can have many of them existing simultaneously throughout the various universes.

There is a direct parallel between Hindu and Buddhist higher body concepts, although the Buddhist uses the idea of higher bodies to cover a greater realm of experience. The difference between the two traditions lies partly in emphasis; whether the bodies already exist and need only to be recognized, or, as in the Buddhist system, only the seed exists from which the higher bodies can slowly be developed.[5] It is possible that both are correct, but the emphasis is clearly different. In either case it is the task of yoga to activate these higher bodies in whatever manner seems best, according to the traditions of the practitioners.

In the highest Buddhist tantras great emphasis is placed on attaining what is called the "illusory body." The great sage Nagarjuna stated that "to become a buddha you must attain a buddha's form body and the illusory body is its primary or substantial cause."[6] Some authorities say that the subtle body and the illusory body are equivalent. Others believe that the illusory body arises out of subtle body experiences. Either way, the basic importance of the connection is indicated.

SPECIAL ASPECTS OF TANTRIC BUDDHISM

Beyond these higher body conceptions there were certain aspects of tantric Buddhism that were unique to the Himalayan kingdoms, particularly in Tibet. The first of these is the "Chod," a highly vivid and somewhat barbaric ritual in which the practitioner calls on deities and demons to eat him alive as a means of attaining total purification.[7] There are various forms of this practice, none of which are gentle. Some authorities believe the Chod is an integration of early Bon practices with tantric Buddhism, which may account for its unique character. Bon was the ancient shamanistic religion that pre-dated Buddhism in Tibet.

A second unique conception is the "tulku," a kind of immortal religious leader. While belief in reincarnation is widespread throughout the Orient, in Tibet a remarkable extension of the concept was made with unique implications for the stability of that country's religious life. Traditional Tibetans believed that high lamas could be reborn by choice as part of their Bodhisattva vows and that suitable tests might be used to recognize their return when they were still young children. Thus it is the same essential Dalai Lama or Karmapa recurring endlessly through time as an act of conscious sacrifice. Obviously, if one accepts this belief, it lends tremendous continuity and stability to the religious line. It constitutes one explanation for the Tibetans' ability to have preserved intact the pure Indian Buddhist tantras from the eighth century into modern times.

A third unique expression of Buddhist traditions is the stupa. As an architectural form the stupa exists in many cultures as a primitive burial mound. Often these monuments were dedicated to powerful chieftains or other important worldly figures. With the coming of Buddhism this form was adopted as a memorial, first of all to the Buddha himself, and then to a variety of other religious and saintly figures. The stupa has assumed many variations in form in different cultures, but certain fundamental elements tend to appear in all of them. Figure 19 presents these elements within a typical Tibetan form.

The stupa is built around a world axis in a manner similar to a Hindu temple. In this case there is an actual pole that runs along the vertical line representing the spine of the construction. The form of the design correspond to the basic constituents of the physical world as understood in the medieval Eastern and Western world: earth, water, fire, air and space. The cube repre-

Fig. 19. Stupa

sents the earth, the sphere is water, the cone is fire, the cap is air and the flaming drop is ether. The five parts of the stupa also represent the base, navel, heart, throat and crown chakras respectively.[8] In essence the stupa is an abstract three-dimensional rendering of the subtle body. As it traditionally contains the ashes of the person to whom it is dedicated, and is built following elaborate rituals intended to balance and perpetuate the energies

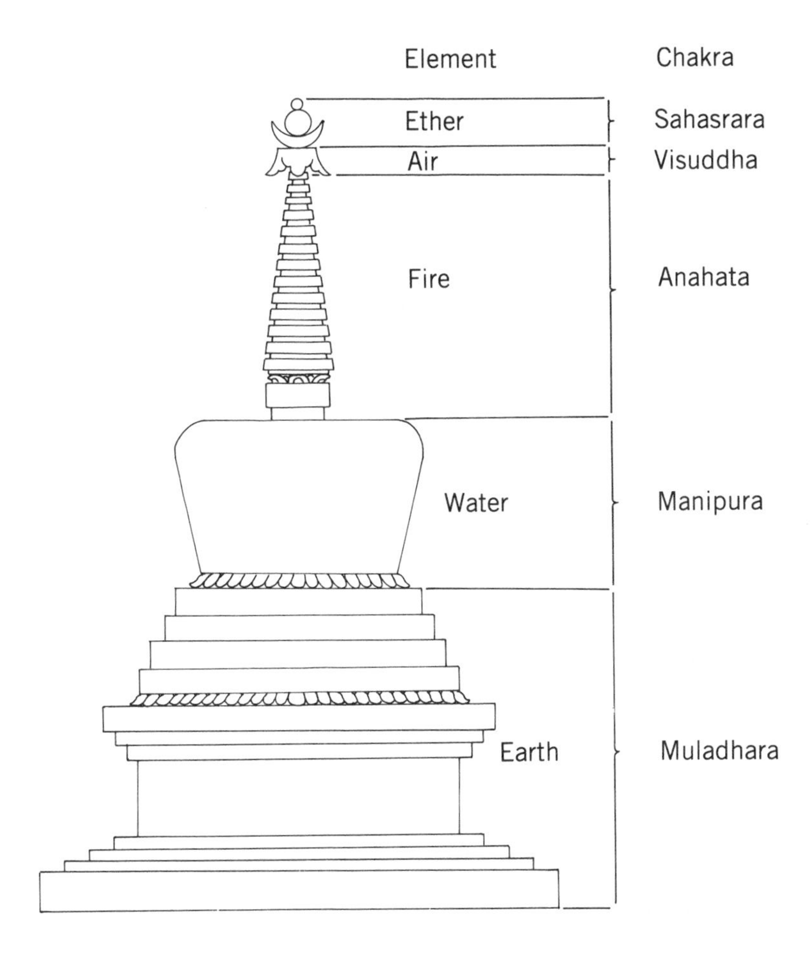

Fig. 20. The 5 elements and the chakra centers in relation to the Stupa structure.

Fig. 21. Stupa "man"

of the Buddhist tradition, it is as if the stupa becomes the energy body of the holy person whose relics it contains. As a result his or her energy continues to radiate influences into the atmosphere after he or she is physically dead. This is further indicated by the human eyes that are painted near the top of certain stupas. Whatever the stupa's history and formal variations from country to country throughout the East, and despite the little that is said about it in many writings, the symbolism that underlies the structure provides clear evidence of the importance of the subtle body within the Buddhist system.

A fourth unusual aspect of Tibetan Buddhism is the extensive use of tantric instruments in various rituals and practices. These instruments are a whole topic unto themselves. They include such objects as scepters, magic daggers, bells, chimes, hooks, choppers, whips, handcuffs and swords. What they all have in common is that they can best be understood as physical representations of energy forms that normally exist in a higher realm. By reproducing them with earthly materials (or sometimes with meteorites from beyond the earth), a contact is established between the higher domain and the lower one. The instruments can then be employed in various rituals where their particular nature serves

Fig. 22. Trantric instruments

to intensify the process. For example, a tantric sword may be used to cut through ignorance. Although such instruments can be applied to the subtle body (for instance, the scepter can be used to feed energy into a chakra), they can be applied to a variety of other functions that have little or nothing to do with the subtle body.

A final unique aspect of tantric Buddhist practice is the "Yidam," a masculine or feminine deity that occupies a central

Fig. 23. Yidam

place in the daily experience of the student. While devotion is universal in religious practice, what is unique about the Yidam is the unlikely combination of love and respect with which it is treated on the one hand, and the sense that the deity is an emanation of one's own being on the other. In Christianity no worshipper would ever think that the Virgin Mary was part of his own deeper nature. But in Buddhist terms everything ultimately returns to the creative void, where deity and human are reduced to the same condition. But even with this belief there is still a need, in the earlier stages of spiritual development, for a guide and higher cosmic companion. In this sense the Yidam becomes the focal point of one's inner experience, and the recipient of all one's efforts. It lives in the student's heart, but appears to be external. The Yidam belongs in the realm of archetypes, not in the everyday world. In a sense it occupies a higher level body with which the student can make contact, and with which he can gradually identify through ritual and prayer. It is immensely reassuring to feel the presence of such a being as the need arises, as a kind of beneficent or wrathful cosmic teacher and companion who takes up where the human guru leaves off.

VAJRAYANA ASPECTS OF SUBTLE BODY PRACTICES

Within the Vajrayana tradition there are three kinds of practices that can be classified as relevant to subtle body work; purification, chakra activation and alchemy. These terms might not be used in Buddhist writings, but they are suitable within the present context because parallels to these categories are found in many other traditions.

A suggestive example of a tantric purification exercise is the Vajrasattva ritual. There are a number of versions of this purification of varying complexity, but even the simplest utilize many of

Fig. 24. Vajrasattva

the typical features of Tantric methodology. These include visualization, sacred sounds, guided daydreams, numerology, interaction with the deity, dissolving into the void and a multidimensional conceptual framework. While the initial description of the ritual might sound complicated, the living experience of performing it flows quite naturally from one stage to the next.

To initiate the purification one visualizes the tantric deity Vajrasattva seated about one's head. Since he is the god of purification in the Buddhist pantheon, this immediately sets the stage for what is to follow. Next one repeats the sacred mantra associated with Vajrasattva 108 times, which causes his heart to overflow with ambrosia that falls on one's head, where it begins to penetrate the brain. One then visualizes that beneath the earth there are all manner of wild animals and demons. One consciously lets go of all the negativity stored in the body while at the same time letting all these creatures free so that they can rise up to consume this pollution, which to them is like perfume. After they are done the ambrosia from Vajrasattva fills each chakra in turn with the radiant energy that originally flowed from his heart. When this is finished one talks to Vajrasattva, asking his forgiveness for all wrong actions one has taken. He responds, hopefully in a friendly manner. One then becomes united with the deity by opening to him. Then everything shrinks to a point until it disappears into the void. This is a simplified version of the basic Vajrasattva purification.

There are various elements in the design of this ritual that do not relate to subtle body practice, such as the mantra and the interaction with the deity. But the introduction of ambrosia into each of the chakras is definitely relevant. And in a broader sense the whole process of purification sets the stage for subtle body work by eliminating unnecessary obstacles for the energy flow that is to follow.

An example of the activation of a chakra in tantric Buddhism is provided by the process of inner inspection. One begins by imagining that one is shrinking so that it is possible to enter the

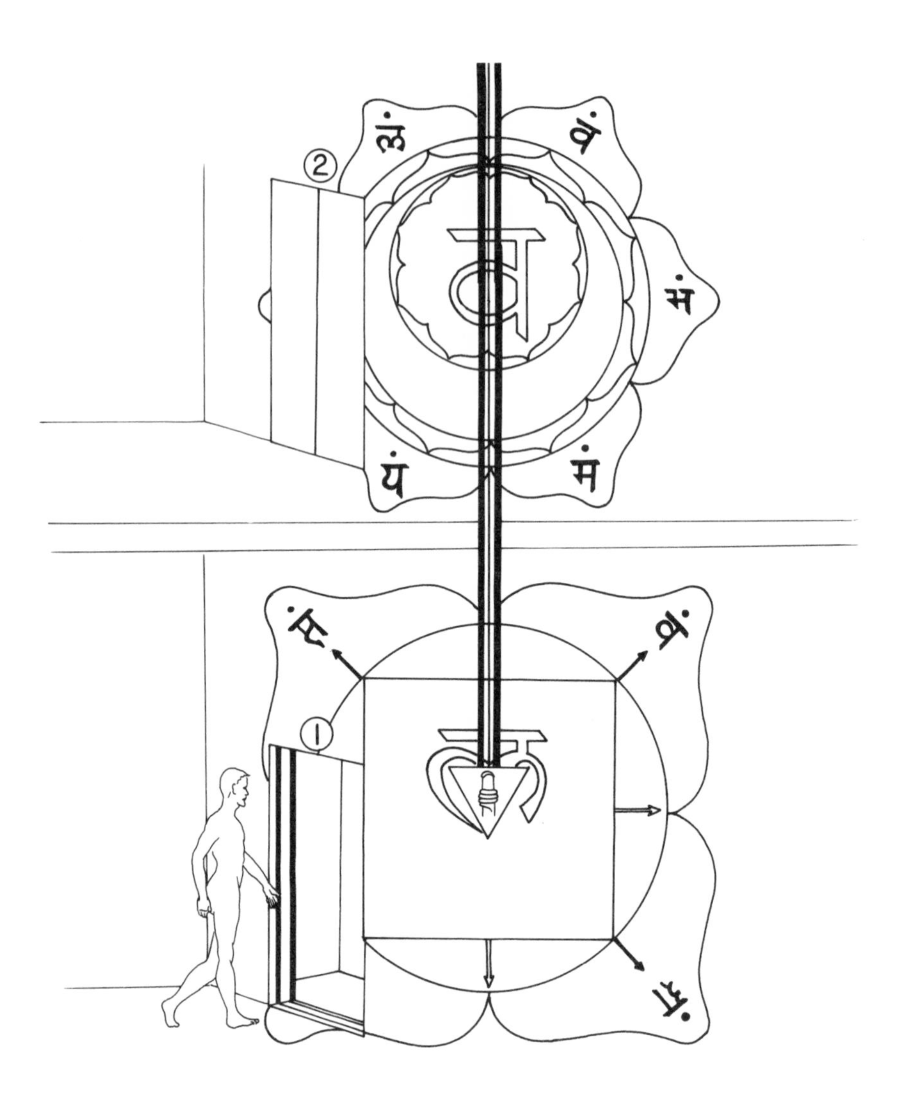

Fig. 25. The "kundalini elevator"

body and move about freely. The purpose is not to inspect the physical body, but rather to explore the subtle body.

One way to begin is to imagine that you enter an elevator in the central channel of the body at the lowest floor. You rise until you reach the level of the next chakra, at which point you step out and look around. Once you are oriented you begin to explore, moving down each petal in turn, noting its color, texture and perspective. At the conclusion of the inspection you reenter the elevator and proceed upward to the next chakra where the process is repeated until the entire system has been explored. The effect of the experience is to increase one's sense of the reality of the subtle body. This can intensify one's motivation to work further to strengthen and activate its functioning.

The third type of practice is alchemical in nature. It involves a fundamental transformation of energy as part of the process of inner development. An illustration of this type of practice is the Four Joys. This method utilizes dumo breathing, which is a means of creating inner fire in the abdomen. There are many types of dumo practice, but in general one concentrates air and energy in the navel chakra in order to ignite a small, clear flame in that area. Starting the fire is a preliminary but essential step. Once it has been ignited, heat begins to rise through the core of the body. Eventually this causes a white drop to melt in the crown chakra and drip into the throat chakra. The white drop can be thought of as a higher energy essence that has been stored in the brain as the result of previous inner work. Slowly, and with an increasing sense of joy, it passes sequentially into each chakra. When it reaches the sex center it can go no farther, so it reverses its course, ascending finally to the crown chakra from where it had originated. The crucial aspect of this process is the impact that the white drop has on the chakras, which is entirely different from the usual effect of focusing attention on them. The distinction is alchemical, that is, it is produced because of the higher quality of energy that is generated by the dumo fire once it begins to melt the crystallized ambrosia in the crown chakra. As this ambrosia passes through each chakra in turn it nourishes them in a new way. It is like a motor that has been run on crude oil all its life when suddenly,

Fig. 26. Dumo

high test gasoline becomes available. The subjective experience is one of bliss.

DIFFERENCES BETWEEN HINDU AND BUDDHIST SUBTLE BODY MODELS

In the preceding examples, terms such as the central or core channel have been used. The reader may have assumed that it was the core of the spine that was meant, as would be the case in the Hindu model. But that would not be true. In *Clear Light of Bliss*[9], a precise model of the subtle body is given from the tantric Buddhist viewpoint. As in the Hindu approach there are three main channels, but there the resemblance ends. The major channel goes up the central axis of the body, a little nearer the back than

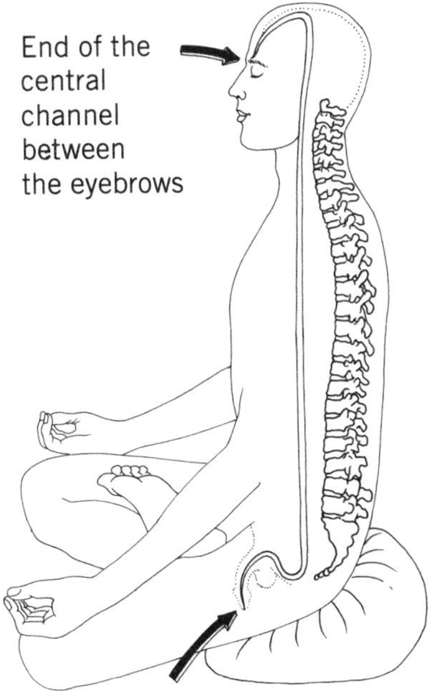

Fig. 27. Central channel

Fig. 28. The side channels

the front, but definitely not in or even near the spine. This central channel follows a straight line except at the top of the head where, after reaching the crown, it arches over and terminates between the eyebrows. At the lower end it stops at the tip of the sexual organ. On either side are two other channels that also move in a straight line, except at the level of the navel, heart, throat and head where they cross over and create a kind of knot.

The contrast in placement of the major channel between the Hindu and Buddhist systems is too striking to be overlooked. On the other hand, each group has done a fairly effective job of avoiding the obvious question; how can they both be right? Hindu writers belonging to an earlier tradition are inclined to ignore the contradiction rather than attempting to solve it. Buddhists have used other approaches. They have, as in *Clear Light of Bliss*, simply assumed that theirs was the correct way and not considered any alternatives. Or they have, as in the writings of Yogi Chen[10] explicitly stated that they are right and the Hindus are wrong. Or they have looked for earlier similarities. Lama Govinda[11], for example, believes that Buddhists are truer to the traditions of Patanjali, one of the codifiers of modern yoga, than are the Hindus. Specifically, he suggests that Patanjali stated that the Ida and Pingala follow a straight line rather than a spiral as Hindus believe. A modern Canadian lama, Namgyal Rinpoche, has the interesting view that it is one's inner experience that counts[12]. Traditional descriptions, whether of the location of channels or the nature of chakras, can become a stumbling block to the mind, particularly if one artificially forces one's experience to conform to them. But the contradiction between the Buddhist and Hindu views of channel locations remains puzzling. It is as if there were two anatomies.

Unfortunately, that is just the beginning. The Buddhist description of the chakras themselves is no less complex than the Hindus. For example, in the *Clear Light Of Bliss*[13] the heart chakra is described as having eight spokes going in the eight directions that one sees in a mandala. Each of these spokes carries a different kind of energy that includes the basic elements (earth, water, fire and air) as well as basic sense experiences (form, smell, taste and touch). Each of these channels splits into three more, so that there are a total of 24 channels organized into three groups of eight, each of which has its own color, type of energy and particular destination. The splitting continues until 72,000 channels are obtained, all having their point of origin in the heart.

A fairly complete description of the chakras according to the Buddhist tantric tradition is given in the recent book *Tibetan*

TABLE 2
The Buddhist Description of The Chakras

	Head	Throat	Heart	Navel	Genitals
Name	Bliss	Enjoyment	Phenomena	Transmutation	Happiness
Number of Spokes	32	16	8	64	32
Bija	OM	AH	HUM	SWA	HA
Color	White	Red	Blue	Yellow	Green
Element	Space	Fire	Water	Earth	Air
Direction	Center	West	East	South	North
Buddha Family	Buddha	Padma	Vajra	Ratna	Karma
Dhyani Buddha	Vairocana	Amitabha	Akshobhya	Ratnasambhava	Amoghasiddi
Buddha Aspect	Body	Speech	Mind	Quality	Activity
Vehicle	Lion	Peacock	Elephant	Horse	Shang Bird
Skandha	Forms	Perceptions	Consciousness	Feelings	Concepts
Poison	Ignorance	Ignorance	Anger	Pride	Jealousy
Wisdom	Absolute Wisdom	Discriminating	Mirror-like	Equalizing	All-accomplishing
Gland	Pineal & Pituitary	Thyroid	Adrenal	Pancreas	Gonads

Buddhist Medicine and Psychiatry by Terry Clifford[14]. A good deal of this material is summarized in table 2.

Some of the categories that are covered in this table are similar to those used in the Hindu tradition. Others, such as "Buddha Family" and "Dhyani Buddha" are not. Table 3 compares the

TABLE 3

A Comparison of Hindu and Buddhist Chakra Descriptions

		Throat	Heart	Navel	Genitals
Number & Petals	*Hindu*	16, purple	12, Bandhuka flower	10, red	6, vermillion
	Buddhist	16, red	8, blue	64, yellow	32, green
Bija	*Hindu*	HAM	YAM	RAM	VAM
	Buddhist	AH	HUM	SWA	HA
Element	*Hindu*	Space	Air	Fire	Water
	Buddhist	Fire	Water	Earth	Air
Function	*Hindu*	Nurturance	Emotions	Burning impurities	Survival
	Buddhist	Speech & Perception	Mind	Feelings	Activity
Vehicle	*Hindu*	Elephant	Antelope	Bull	Gurada
	Buddhist	Peacock	Elephant	Horse	Shang bird

Buddhist and Hindu chakra descriptions using the categories and chakras that they share in common. The chakras in the head are not included because the Buddhists combine them whereas the Hindus do not.

The major conclusion to be drawn from an inspection of table 3 is that there is virtually no similarity in the descriptions of the chakras in the two traditions. The only exception is that in both systems the throat chakra has 16 petals, although the colors are different. Also, in the sex chakra the vehicles are both birds, although of different kinds.

One wonders whether it is the same set of chakras that are being described. One possibility is that they are not—that is, there are different chakras in the spine than in the core channel. However, no one has ever claimed that this was the case. Perhaps it is mostly a question of spiritual politics, each tradition developing their own version of reality in a realm that is basically visionary in nature. Perhaps the Buddhists have gone to extremes, making as many contrasts as possible to differentiate themselves from their Hindu context. Of course they would be unlikely to admit it.

Another possibility is that these descriptions represent different mystical experiences of particular individuals that over time have become crystallized into a tradition that others follow, forcing their own experience to conform with those of their masters.

Perhaps each system expresses these matters in its own terms while assuming they are universal. Thus Hindu deities appear in Hindu subtle bodies, just as Christian beings exist in a Christian heaven. How could it be otherwise? And yet how could it be that way? Does each religion pray to a different creator? Ultimately it cannot be, although each religion is, in a sense, a separate creation.

While it is easy to ask these questions, it is difficult to answer them. And, in any case, it is disturbing to have parallel traditions describe what is apparently the same thing in such a different manner, while still continuing to take the reality of the subtle body seriously. And yet, if one separates all the contradictions from what is fundamental, there seems little doubt that the subtle body is of basic importance in the understanding of spiritual development as it is conceived in these two traditions. Simply ignoring the specifics because they are contradictory is not a responsible action. Even if the knot is difficult to unravel, it is necessary to make the effort.

In summary, Buddhism is a kind of "three layer cake", growing originally as a reform movement within Hinduism and continuing to develop and refine over the centuries. Unlike Hinduism, it is a missionary religion, which accounts for its spread throughout the East.

While it is possible to read many books on Buddhism without encountering the slightest mention of a chakra or a channel, there is reason to believe that the subtle body plays an important part in its higher yogic practices. Although the Buddhist description of the chakras and the channels is almost entirely different from that of the Hindu tradition, the basic sense of ascending from the base through higher and higher levels of experience, culminating in the crown, is directly parallel. Overall, the comparison between the two traditions has raised many more questions than it has resolved.

CHAPTER FOUR

THE TAOIST APPROACH

Until quite recently Westerners considered Taoism to be either philosophical or superstitious. The philosophical orientation is most clearly illustrated by the classic text of Taoism, the *Tao Te Ching* by Lao Tze, written about the time of the historical Buddha. Consider its opening lines:

> The Tao that can be told of
> Is not the Absolute Tao;
> The names that can be given
> Are not Absolute Names.
> The Nameless is the origin of Heaven and Earth;
> The Named is the Mother of All Things.[1]

The whole sense of Taoism breathes from these simple but profoundly reverberating lines. There are no deities and no hierarchy, just the acceptance of the underlying mystery of reality as it reveals itself through the growing stillness of our own contemplation.

In religious history it is generally assumed that the early high water mark in the development of Taoism was followed by a gradual decay in which a priesthood functioned in a climate of superstition and magic. In order to popularize the religion, which had to compete with the highly colorful Buddhism that had recently arrived from India, they embraced much of what had previously been ignored or rejected in China; a vast pantheon of deities. Unlike Buddhism, where a similar development occurred, this did not lead to an expansion and enrichment of the tradition within a tantric framework. The tendency was rather to create a split between the depth contained in the Taoist mystical tradition and the more magical, worldly aspects of Folk Taoism. The latter became more prominent and Folk Taoism came to be regarded with mild disdain by cultured Chinese trained in the Confucian tradition.

One of the first indications in the west that Taoism might have a quite different aspect was the publication in 1967 of *The Secret of the Golden Flower*[2]. With an introduction by Carl Jung, this work gave clear evidence of an esoteric Taoist tradition. Its major principles were contained in the phrases "reversing the flow" and "circulating the light." To the casual reader these phrases may have been less than illuminating, but in the context of the subtle body practices of Buddhists and Hindus, they represented fundamental principles. Circulating the light is a basic premise of subtle body work, while reversing the flow describes the direction that needs to be taken; that is, instead of losing energy to the outer world through the heart, throat, sexual organ and mind, an effort must be made to absorb energy and circulate it internally to feed one's inner nature. This is most clearly seen in relation to sexual energy, which all esoteric traditions emphasize must be refined for higher development, rather than used only as a vehicle for human pleasure and reproduction.

THE NATURE OF TAOIST YOGA

More recently a whole new aspect of these teachings has begun to become available in the West under the heading of Taoist Yoga. The purpose of yoga, whether Hindu, Buddhist or Taoist, is to provide a collection of methods for achieving inner development and higher consciousness. These methods, while influenced by the cultural and mystical traditions of their practitioners, represent the crystallized experiences of those who have devoted their lives to personal evolution.

Taoist Yoga is essentially Chinese. While it has been infused with poetic imagery and endless mystical terminology, it is ultimately practical. The poetic aspect is easily illustrated. In *The Secret of the Golden Flower*, for example, it is stated that:

> When the light is allowed to move in a circle, all the powers of Heaven and Earth, of the Light and the Dark, are crystallized. This is what is described as seedlike, or purification of the power, or purification of the concept.[3]

Such a description is striking but less than totally clear in its abstraction, although this kind of obscure language is not unique to the Chinese. Buddhist tantrics often purposely leave their scriptures incomplete, so that only a teacher can fill in the gaps. The early initiations were called "whispered" because that is how they were given to the students who were considered worthy to receive them. In Hinduism similar practices were pursued. The relation between Guru and student was considered sacred, and nothing that was disclosed in private could be revealed without express permission. By keeping the vital elements in the teacher's hands, the transmission process could be controlled. Also, secrecy had a certain appeal. It motivated students to achieve an understanding beyond that available to others. Furthermore, it prevented information and principles from being learned before they could be properly understood and utilized.

Taoism claims a history of over 5,000 years, although more conservative scholars' estimates are about half that length. It is, in any case, a long development and constitutes the repository of a vast amount of personal experience of the sages who devoted their lives to its practice. There are over 1,200 volumes in the Taoist Canon.

Taoism has three major aspects which roughly parallel those found in Hinduism and Buddhism; purification, developing the subtle body and spiritual alchemy. The harmonizing and purifying aspect has been elaborately developed with emphasis upon circulation of subtle body energy within the physical body.

A simple example is the Inner Smile exercise.[4] It is based on the observation that perhaps the most immediate and accessible form of positive healing energy for the average person is a sincere smile. In the Inner Smile exercise the energy associated with smiling is taken step by step throughout the body until every organ, bone and blood vessel is smiling—that is, expressing the energy associated with a smiling condition.

In some ways this exercise is like starting a fire. First one must gather kindling and light it. Then one adds branches and logs. This is the equivalent of finding a sincere smile inside and beginning to spread it to different bodily structures, such as the right eye, left eye, chin, the scalp, various endocrine glands, bones, nerves and so on. The important thing is to proceed gradually. If too much is done prematurely, the energy will be dispersed and the smiling fire will be extinguished. But the further you go, the easier it is to spread the energy.

The purpose of this exercise is to create a harmonized and happy condition within the organism. This is, in a sense, its own reward. It is also an excellent preparation for any deeper form of subtle body practice, and constitutes a characteristic Taoist approach to purification.

While Hindu yogis work toward union with the infinite and Buddhists seek oblivion of the self, Taoists usually aim for immortality in the form of a spiritual body made of energies crystallized from their physical and energy bodies. This has led them to be

Fig. 29. The inner smile

somewhat more concerned with the state of their physical well-being and has fostered some significant side developments in the areas of medicine and martial arts.

MARTIAL ARTS AND ACUPUNCTURE

Spiritual practices involving lengthy seated meditation often render adepts less able to defend themselves against hostile social forces. In the unsettled conditions of medieval China it gradually became evident that monks had to develop martial arts to protect not only their communities but themselves when they traveled or went into isolated retreat in areas with wild animals. Some authorities trace martial arts development to the sixth century, with the coming of Boddhidarma from India to China. He was interested in developing exercises for monks who otherwise sat in quiet meditation all day. Since that time, all of the deeper martial arts traditions contain a spiritual aspect. For example, in Aikido, a twentieth century Japanese development, "ki" is emphasized as the vital cosmic energy without which the various techniques cannot work properly. Similarly, in the widespread Chinese art of Tai Chi Chuan, "chi" has exactly the same function. It flows within and energizes the various Tai Chi movements until one reaches the "supreme ultimate".

Medical developments such as acupuncture grew out of the Taoist practitioners' need to perfect their physical health. While their goal was similar to that of Hatha Yoga, the methods differed. An early Taoist yogi[5] became particularly concerned with the elimination of energy blocks in various subtle body channels, both in himself and in his students. He conceived of the idea of using gold and silver needles to draw the body's awareness to specific areas that were congested as an alchemical aid in opening the channels. His interest was purely yogic and spiritual. It was some time before this method spread to the broader population. It was used to treat a vast number of medical conditions, eventually giving rise to acupuncture as we know it today. It is the spread of acupuncture that has helped to familiarize Western readers with complex road-maps of energy circuits in the human body, such as the one shown in figure 30.

There are an endless number of such illustrations in the Taoist medical literature. The reader can be forgiven if he is confused about what is being represented. It is relatively easy to assume that these maps refer to a level of understanding different from the subtle body, particularly when you read about meridians and pressure points that are used to explain the diagrams. It is difficult

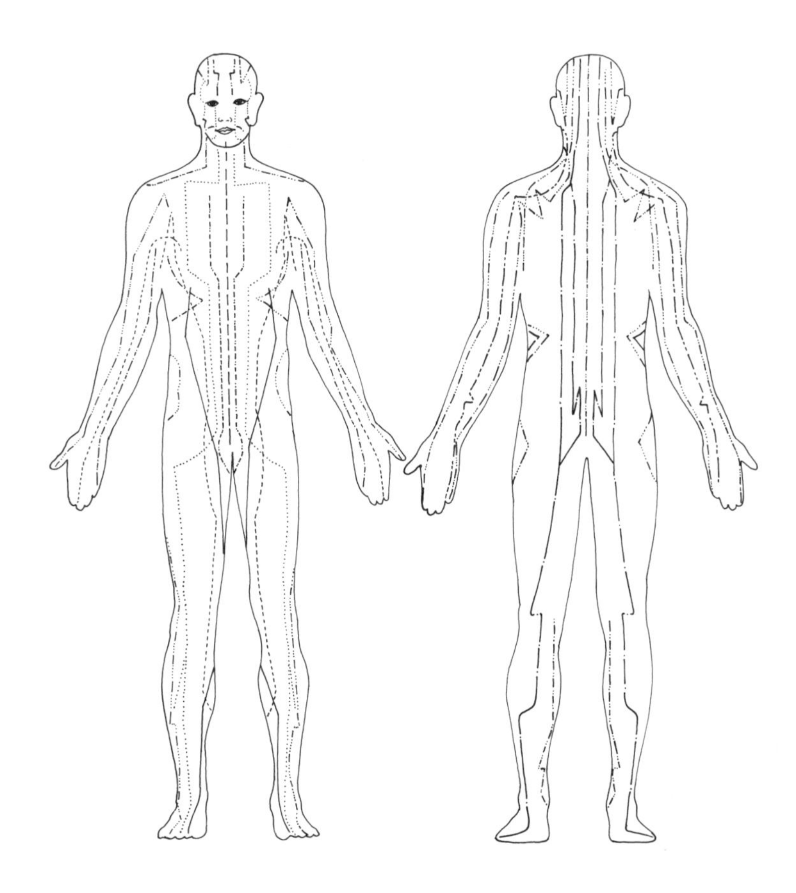

Fig. 30. The 12 main meridians of acupuncture

to detect the relatively simple chakra system in the endless anatomical complexity of the energy channels of Chinese medicine.

But on closer inspection one sees some familiar correspondences related to the chakras and the main and subsidiary channels. This suggests that we may be dealing with a more detailed and complex map of partially familiar territory, created for a somewhat different purpose than that pursued by yoga. Acupuncture diagrams attempt to locate all spots where channel connections occur and blockages could exist. These have diagnostic and therapeutic usefulness from a medical viewpoint. For the yogi, starting with a very healthy organism, such detailed precision may be unnecessary.

Once it is understood that these Chinese road-maps are more complete diagrams of the subtle body (and both Hindu and Buddhist systems state that there are 72,000 energy channels), the relation of these maps to Taoist yoga and alchemy becomes much clearer, particularly their relation to the 12 major acupuncture meridians and the eight special psychic channels that are often described in them. Charles Luk[6], for example, states that the practitioner, on awakening in the morning, circulates vital energy originating at the base of the sex organs through all the eight major channels of the body as a kind of basic subtle body stretching exercise.

In Taoist Yoga there is, in addition, extensive use of the "three tantiens" which have a direct relation to the chakras. The tantiens are used for storing three types of energy; sexual, vital and spiritual, and are located in the naval, heart and head respectively. They are not so much places where channels connect as they are major storage areas. Their locations correspond to the chakras situated in the core channel in those same areas.

In more advanced alchemical practices, the functioning of the

Fig. 31. Steaming process

subtle body and its various channels and storage areas is assumed. One example of such a method is "steaming." In the Taoist system heat is associated with the heart center, while moist coolness is related to the lower "tantien" or "sea of energy," located in the lower abdomen. In order to initiate the steaming process, cool energies contained in the kidneys and genitals are accumulated at the base of the trunk, while hot energies located in the heart and head are stored in the heart center. The watery, cool energies are brought up one subsidiary channel, while the hot energies are brought down another. It is called reversing "Kan" and "Li" (or fire and water).

The fire is carefully placed under the water, which is drawn into a cauldron that is visualized in the core channel at the level of the navel. The cauldron is heated until steaming gradually begins to take place. This steam has the power to purify and germinate various organs and energy centers in the body to prepare the way for higher processes to begin to function. This alchemical procedure utilizes not only the base and heart centers, but also the core and subsidiary channels, and to this extent is a subtle body exercise.

THE TAOIST MODEL OF THE SUBTLE BODY

The basic elements in the Taoist spiritual anatomy, as in the Hindu and Buddhist, are the energy centers and the channels that connect them. The most important of these are located in the core,

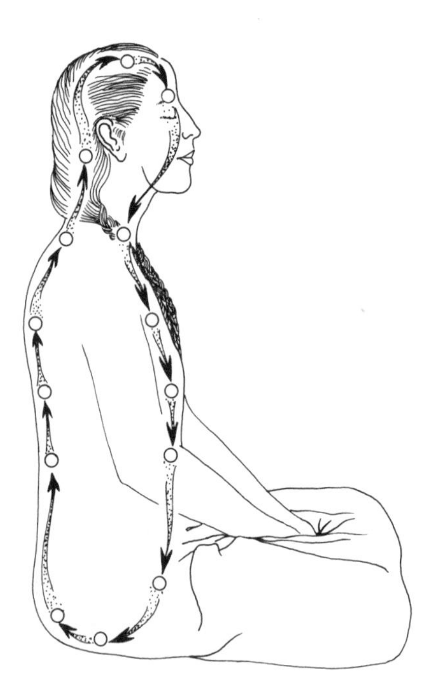

Fig. 32. The microcosmic orbit

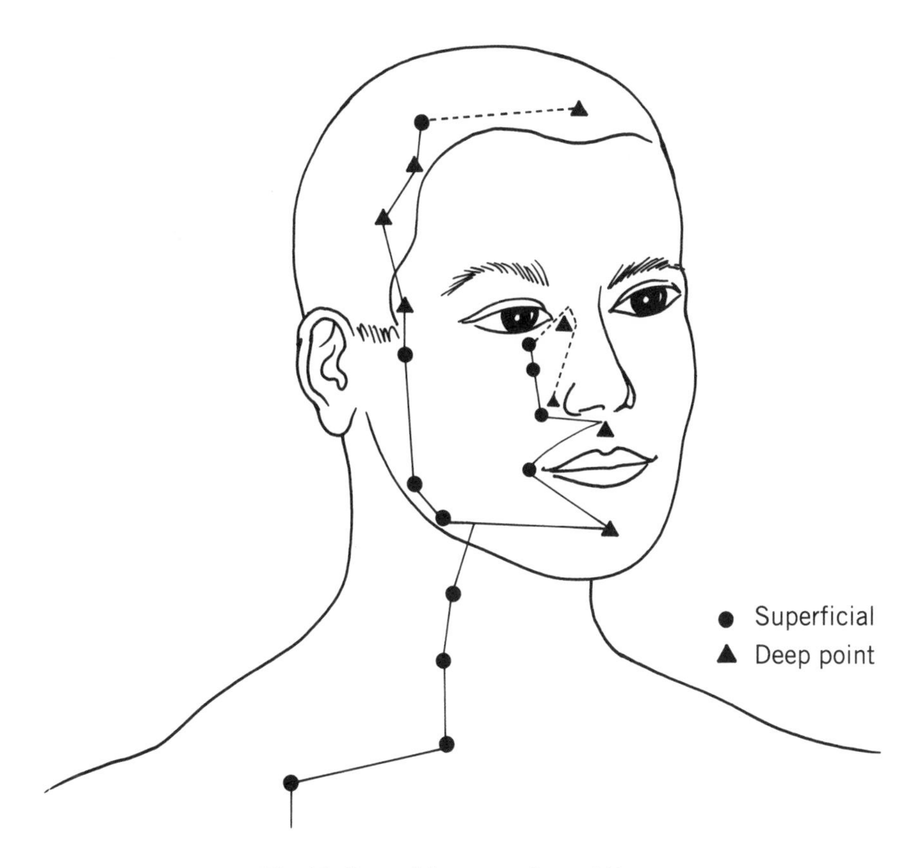

Fig. 33. Part of the stomach meridian

up the back and down the front of the midline of the body. The central core channels correspond to those in the tantric Buddhist model used for transforming subtle energies into spiritual energies. The channel in the spine corresponds to the Hindu model. The channel along the front of the body, in combination with the one in the back, constitutes the Microcosmic Orbit, which forms an inner system for digesting and circulating energies of various types.

In addition, five other major channels are distinguished as among the major tributaries of the subtle body. These are the positive arm channel, negative arm channel, positive leg channel, negative leg channel and the belt channel that winds around the body. There are also 24 meridian channels, 12 on each side of the body, namely: the spleen, liver, kidney, pericardium, heart, stomach, gall bladder, large intestine, small intestine, triple warmer meridians and the Bridge and Regulator channels which link together all the meridians of the body.

Each of these energy pathways is defined by pressure points associated with the practice of acupuncture. It is difficult to precisely describe the path of a particular channel since one must locate it in an organic, three dimensional solid. But if one can identify the specific energy points that define the channel, the process of internal identification becomes much easier.

For example, to say that part of the stomach meridian runs across the lower portion of the jaw and ascends by the front of the ear following the hairline to the forehead does not clearly locate its position. To draw a two dimensional diagram is more helpful. But if one focuses on each of the points shown in figure 33 and can feel their presence as an organic sensation, it becomes comparatively easy to identify the channel that connects them.

There is a distinct contrast between the Buddhist and Hindu conceptions of the chakras and that of the Taoists. Instead of a central channel containing elaborately developed chakras, each with their own unique mythology and symbolism as in Hinduism and Buddhism, in Taoism there are 32 major channels containing numerous chakras that are looked upon as so many buds that can bloom if enough attention is given to them. In a sense, there are as many buds as there are pressure points. Most modern acupuncturists use the points somewhat mechanically. They do not see them as accessing different dimensions of experience, nor do they associate the points with any highly developed symbolism.

This mechanical orientation is not found in traditional acupuncture, where the subtle energy connections to each organ are carefully detailed along with an elaborate set of associations to colors, animals, directions, emotions, and so on. Table 4 summarizes some of these associations. Their complexity is reminiscent of the chakra associations in Hinduism and Buddhism. Taoists claim to have identified the most complete set of roadmaps for the circuitry of the subtle body. Looking at some of the charts contained in classic Chinese texts on the subject, the impression is confirmed.

None of these maps are in direct contradiction to the Hindu and Buddhist conception of the 72,000 nadis. There are more than enough nadis to cover the complexity of the acupuncture channels.

TABLE 4

Taoist Associations with the Five Organs

	Heart	Lung	Kidney	Liver	Spleen
Element	Fire	Metal	Water	Wood	Earth
Season	Summer	Autumn	Winter	Spring	—
Direction	South	West	North	East	—
Sense Organ	Tongue	Nose	Ear	Eyes	Mouth
Taste	Bitter	Pungent	Salty	Sour	Sweet
Color	Red	White	Blue-Black	Green	Yellow
Animal	Phoenix	Tiger	Turtle	Dragon	Dragon
Emotion:					
Negative	Cruelty	Grief	Fear	Anger	Imbalance
Positive	Respect	Dignity	Gentleness	Kindness	Equlibrium

TAOIST ALCHEMY

Beyond the energy circuitry and chakra buds, there is an elaborate system of Taoist alchemy designed to generate higher bodies. Both Hinduism and Buddhism also emphasize such work. In Taoism the relation between the bodies is made particularly clear. Table 5 makes a direct comparison between the systems.

Hinduism tends to assume the existence of these bodies, whereas Buddhism and Taoism believe that it is only through arduous inner work that they can be developed. Taoism takes the interesting view that higher bodies must be formed by a kind of internal intercourse, in a direct parallel to human physical reproduction. This process is taken quite literally.

After successful internal fertilization, nine months are required before birth and up to 20 years before a mature higher body can be successfully cultivated. The result is a pure energy body that in turn forms a stepping stone for the development of the immortal body or the spirit. The fact that it takes so long to form the energy body may be a little confusing since Taoists are dealing with energy channels and centers from the beginning, but these are viewed as existing within the physical body and intimately related to it. The energy body, when it has been successfully formed, is an independent creation, rather similar to the Illusory

TABLE 5
A Comparison of Higher Bodies

Hinduism	Buddhism	Taoism
Physical	Emanation	Physical
Subtle	Enjoyment	Soul
Cosmic	Truth	Spirit

Fig. 34. The Taoist three bodies

Body in advanced tantric Buddhism. In any case, it is made crystal clear in the Taoist system that the soul or energy body must be created before the spirit or immortal body can develop. It constitutes the crucial intervening link in the development of the higher immortal body, to which the individual can turn after death as a permanent vehicle for his further exploration of the universe, and whose creation is the ultimate objective of his spiritual work.

An interesting example of the integration of different levels of inner development in Taoism is found in the "Fusion of the Five Elements" process. While the methods associated with the fusion process will be given in greater detail in Part II, the basic principles can be previewed here[7].

Fusion is essentially a unification of the five elements (water, fire, metal, wood and earth) within the body. The initial part of this process involves the purification of emotional energies utilizing all three bodies. It focuses on the organs of the physical body that are the storage sites of various negative emotions, and uses the cosmic or space body that is associated with only higher positive qualities. And, as an intervening link, it employs the subtle body as the vehicle in which the fusion process actually takes place.

The Taoists associate the kidneys with fear, the liver with anger, the heart with cruelty, the spleen with worry and imbalance and the lungs with grief; that is, these negative emotions tend to be stored in those organs. In the fusion process the emotions are redirected to storage points in the subtle body and then fused in the navel into a higher and more balanced energy. Then, in the final stage, the purified energies are returned to the organs from which they originated. Fear has been changed to gentleness, anger to kindness, cruelty to respect, imbalance to equilibrium, and grief to dignity. What started as lower negative emotions have become higher cosmic qualities in a process utilizing aspects of all three bodies.

In summary, while Taoism has created elaborate maps of the energy circuitry of the subtle body, it is far less detailed in its description of the chakras than Hinduism or Buddhism. The

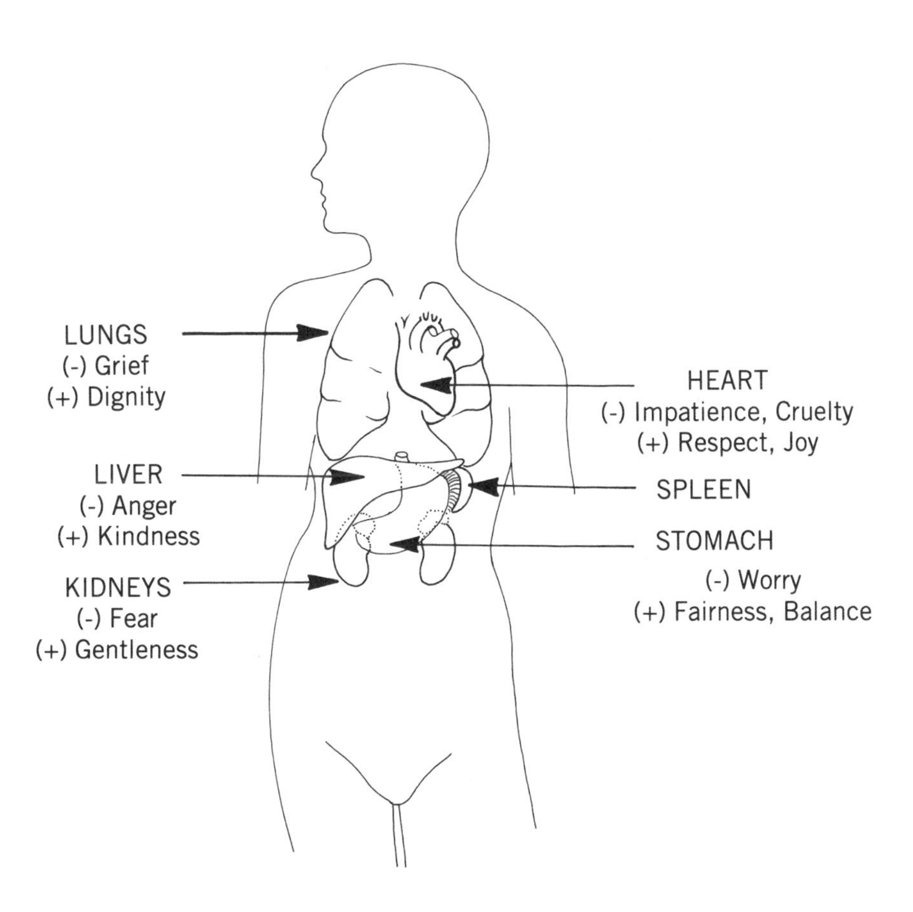

Fig. 35. The negative and positive emotions associated with bodily organs.

complexity and subtlety of Taoist yoga is a recent rediscovery in the West. It places the more familiar tantric practices into a new perspective and indicates how wide-spread these type of subtle body practices were in the ancient East.

CHAPTER FIVE

OTHER TRADITIONS

Within most cultures there are indications of the subtle body concept. In the East these forms are ancient and sophisticated. In a number of third world countries in the Middle East, Africa and South America, the model is more difficult to detect, while in the West its development has been inhibited by our scientific orientation. Nevertheless, if one looks, the traces are usually discernible.

Perhaps the simplest approach is to search for the recognition of a higher life force within each culture, which the subtle body utilizes in the process of transformation. In an article on this subject in *The Psychic Observer*[1], 49 different instances drawn from many cultures, ancient and modern, are given. These include: Mana (Polynesians), Vis Medicatrix Naturae (ancient Greeks), Vital Fludi (medieval alchemists), Ranaa (Hindus), Manna (Israelites), Ka (Egyptians), Astral Light (Kabbalists), Baraka (Sufis), Mungo (Africans), Chi (Chinese), Kerei (Indonesians), Tondi (Sumatrans), Blima (Belgian Congo), Numen (Romans), El (Hebrews), Ki (Japanese), and a variety of terms from American Indians, such as Orenda (Iroquoi), Manitou (Algonquian), Waken (Siox), Wakonda (Omaha), Maxpe (Crow), Digin (Navaho), Dige (Apache) and Hullo (Chicasaw).

In modern systems one finds parallel terms such as: Biotronics, Bioplasma, Ethertricity, Cosmo-electric Energy, Biocosmic Energy, and last but not least, the Orgone Energy identified by Dr. Wilhelm Reich. Considering the universality of the life force concept, it is incredible that Dr. Reich was persecuted by the United States government and ultimately put into federal prison for teaching people to relate to just this type of energy. It is an event that seems more and more ironic with the passage of time.

In any case, the recognition of an underlying life force animating nature is a necessary, but not sufficient, condition for the functioning of the subtle body. There must also be an acknowledgment of energy centers and channels within the body through which the life force can flow.

THE SPREAD OF THE SUBTLE BODY CONCEPT

Evidence for the recognition of chakras is widely dispersed. Perhaps the most striking example of such separation is found among the Kalahari Bushman and the Australian Aborigines, since communication between these cultures has been virtually non-existent.

In 1973 Katz[2] described how the Kung people of the Kalahari desert in Africa utilized dance in order to produce a kundalini type of experience. They believed that the basic life force resided in the pit of the stomach. As it was stirred up by the dance it rose up the spine to the head, where a transcendent state was produced. This temporary condition was characterized by such special powers as seeing at a great distance, x-ray vision and the ability to heal members of the tribe. They sought this state both for their own development and in order to help others. In their society it was not considered an exceptional state, and Katz reported that over half the members of the tribe had known the experience. It is remarkable that a condition almost unknown in the West and rare in the East can become a fairly predictable event in the proper cultural context. But this does not mean that the Kung take it for granted. Each session was viewed as a heroic encounter by the tribesmen which involved overcoming inner fear and various kinds of physical resistance.

At the other end of the earth are the Australian Aborigines, long geographically separated from the rest of humanity. Even in modern times they have been able to maintain many of their ancient traditions in spite of Western colonization. Perhaps best known for their concept of "dream time", they are also quite familiar with the importance of the lower belly as the center of human vitality. While studying the Aborigines in the field, Dr. Harvey Wasserman[3] asked, based only on his intuition, whether a particular ritual he was observing required them to connect with the center in the lower belly. The natives' response was one of amazement, as they said; "White man knows nothing of force in belly!" It was as much a surprise for them to be questioned about the center as it was for Dr. Wasserman to have his intuition confirmed.

Native American cultures, North and South, widely recognize the importance of the life force, but the utilization of chakras has not been so obvious. Frank Waters has recently clarified the situation. Writing about his experiences with various southwestern Indian tribes, he concludes:

> The seven ravines of the Quiche Maya, the seven womb caverns of the Aztecs, the seven ancestral 'barrancas' of the Tarahumaras, the seven caves of the Hopis, the seven womb-caves of the Zunis, and the seven ancestral villages of the Yaquis—all these can be equated with the seven psychophysical centers within man himself.[4]

Further, depending on how one interprets the reality of Carlos Castenada's reports of his work with the Yaquis, his material confirms the importance not only of the subtle body in general, but of the lower belly in particular as the site of life force.

In a personal communication Charles Lawrence[5] reports that northwest indian medicine men utilize the central axis of the body in their healing practices. This approach has generally been secret, so that its implication for subtle body practice has not been clear to others.

Furthermore, there are various forms of ceremonial and ritual dress found throughout the world where tradition may have replaced understanding of the subtle body symbolism that is being portrayed.

For example, the Blackfoot Indians wear a spiraling hair arrangement coming out of the forehead, resembling a magician's crest that is associated with higher chakra functioning. The ritual dot worn by Hindu women is clearly symbolic of the third eye. In South Africa a cowrie shell is often worn in the same area. Similar-

Fig. 36. Blackfoot Indian hairdo

Fig. 37. Jewish and Egyption head pieces

ly, the Zulu wear a headdress that brings energy to focus in the area of the third eye. The Yarmulke worn by religious Jews roughly symbolizes the area of the thousand-petaled lotus. The traditional headdress of the Egyptian pharaohs is designed to magnify the energy currents of the higher chakras in the head. The traditional Chinese mandarin gown is overtly symbolic of the degree of political power of the owner. But here the symbolism goes further. The dragon, which represents authority, coils in the area of the belly, while its head rests on the heart center. The owner's body creates the world axis when the garment is worn, and the garment itself establishes a separation between the material world, governed by the dragon robe, and the spiritual realm, represented by the emerging neck and head of the wearer.

CHAKRAS IN CHRISTIANITY

The major traditions of the Western world each provide instances of the utilization of the chakras. The famous but slightly

Fig. 38. "If thine eye be single, they whole body will be full of light."

puzzling statement from the New Testament, "If thine eye be single, thy whole body will be full of light," appears to describe the functioning of the third eye. This statement can be taken as referring to the light of understanding, or to the energy from the atmosphere that can be drawn in through the third eye and become part of the subtle body network, filling the individual with light.

In Christian symbolism[6] the head represents the seat of life, which rules the other members. This concept closely parallels the idea that the lotus chakra contains and communicates with all the other chakras, just as the pituitary contacts and coordinates the hormonal system.

Similarly, the heart in Christian symbolism is clearly associated with love and devotion. Whether the physical heart and the heart center are differentiated is not always clear, but the function is

Fig. 39. The movement of mantra from head to throat to heart.

Fig. 40. The descent of prayer to the three centers.

similar. Furthermore, the heart is viewed as containing the essence of the individual or the most sacred part of him. This is parallel to the practice of showing the object of devotion within the heart of the practitioner in both Eastern and some Western religions.

It is traditional in Christian religious art to portray holy persons and angels with either an aureole, a field of radiance that appears to emerge from and encircle the whole body, or a halo or nimbus that appears behind and around the head of such beings. There are different forms and colors that are used, each with their particular symbolism, but the most striking aspect of these energy forms is that they provide a clear expression of the functioning of the energy body in these people. Purified energy is portrayed as golden, luminous, flame-like or rainbow hued. When the total body is activated it is best portrayed as the aureole. Functions of the higher centers in and around the head are naturally represented by a halo. Christians do not usually explain the use of these energy forms as manifestations of the subtle body, but the implication is clear. Where else would it come from?

Within the Eastern Orthodox tradition additional indications of the subtle body occur. In *The Way of a Pilgrim*[7] the effects of the Jesus Prayer are graphically described. While the contents of the prayer are distinctly Christian ("Lord Jesus Christ, have mercy on me, a sinner"), the principles involved are similar to those employed in mantra yoga; the repetition of sacred words and syllables of special meaning to the individual. Furthermore, through endless repetition the prayer moves from the mind to the throat and finally settles in the heart, where its impact is greatly amplified. This sequence corresponds to the opening of the head, throat and heart chakras, as the energy of the prayer gradually works its way deeper into the individual. The effects of the prayer also bear a direct relation to the Buddhist conception that the fundamental human actions are mind, speech and compassion.

When one passes from traditional Christianity to its more modern esoteric versions, the association of chakras with other practices becomes much more specific. It is hard to determine whether this association is simply created by modern Christians based on their knowledge of Eastern traditions, or comes from an

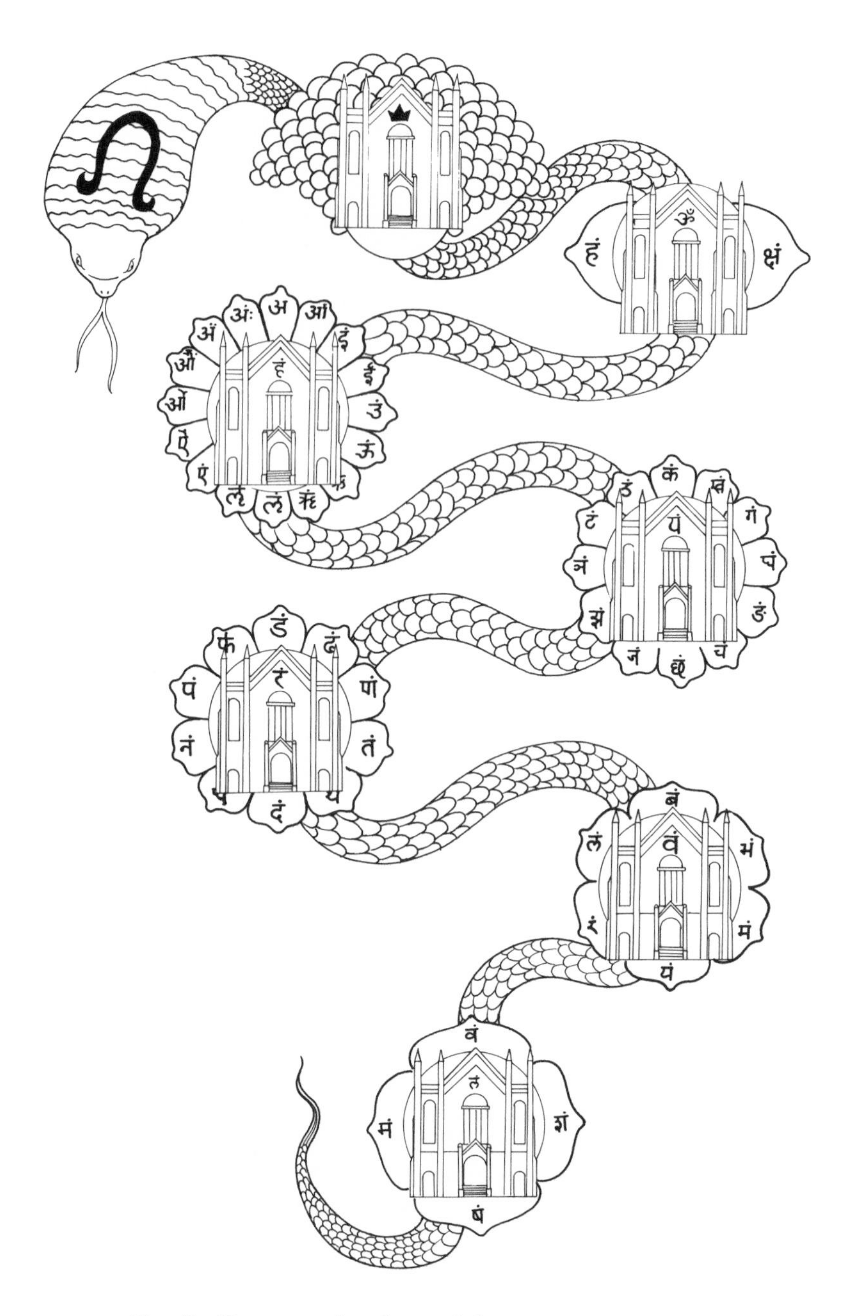

Fig. 41. The seven churches and the seven centers

understanding of hidden aspects of the Christian tradition itself. In either case some mention should be made of this literature.

There is, for example, a commentary on the Book of Revelations by Edgar Cayce[8] that makes a direct connection between the poetic Christian symbolism contained in Revelations and the subtle body. He equates the seven churches with the seven spiritual centers. From there he proceeds to interpret the Book of Revelations as an essentially yogic text, describing how the various energy centers can be purified and integrated so that a new being is created on the level of Christ consciousness.

One of the more influential modern spiritual teachers is George Gurdjieff. His system clearly emphasizes the importance of three centers in the head, the heart and the lower spine. At one point in his lectures he explicitly stated that his teaching could be described as esoteric Christianity.[9]

Another instance of the extensive use of the chakra model within the context of modern christianity is found in the work of Jean Savoy.[10] It is not clear whether Savoy's use of the subtle body is a later addition to his more fundamental biblical studies or an insight derived from them. But there is little doubt that a considerable literature has developed in modern mystical Christianity and spiritualism that assumes and incorporates the subtle body model.

CHAKRAS IN ISLAM

In comparison to Christianity, the Islamic religion is unusually direct. It eliminates the formal clergy, minimizes theology and emphasizes a belief in one God. It appears to have little to say about the subtle body or other forms of higher spiritual expression. But within the Sufi aspects of the tradition, traces and hints can be found.

A particularly interesting and suggestive instance occurs in *The Mystic Rose From the Garden of the King*[11]. This highly poetic manuscript contains a description of a strange temple of knowledge, seven stories high. A careful reading of this portion of the manuscript suggests a reasonable correspondence between the seven levels and the traditional functions of the seven chakras. The third chakra from the bottom, for example, contains a radiant hunter, an unsupported sword representing the need for balance between man and nature, and an aged dervish surrounded by a mantle of protection. These images are in keeping with the function of the navel chakra as the basic balancing point of energy flow and the source of strength and protection.

Furthermore, in the final paragraph of the same work, when the king who is listening to the account of the Mystic Rose asks where the temple of knowledge is to be found, the Mystic Dervish replies, "Turn to thy heart; hidden therein lieth the magnificent Temple of Knowledge," clearly indicating that the vision is internal in its origin and focus.

Occasionally a reference to "latifa" also appears in Sufi literature, which is an equivalent term for "chakra". But since Hindus, Moslems and Sufis have a long history of contact, this is scarcely remarkable.

CHAKRAS IN JUDAISM

The earliest major Middle Eastern tradition that continues to exert an influence in the modern world is Judaism. It is based on the study of the Old Testament, the Torah (a series of commentaries on the Old Testament and other sacred texts), and the Kabbalah. The latter is the repository of the more mystical aspects of the religion. The major symbol of the teachings in the Kabbalah is the Tree of Life, whose basic form is indicated in figure 42.

In some ways the Tree of Life parallels the Hindu Shree Yantra. Both describe the total process of universal creation and incorporate a vast array of parallel concepts, including the identity of the macrocosm and the microcosm.

An inspection of the overall design of the Tree of Life suggests a parallel with the major channels of the subtle body. The central power flows in the vertical axis. The left- and right-hand columns circle in their descent, exactly as do the Ida and Pingala, and are associated with the masculine and feminine aspects of the universe. Furthermore, as one looks at the diagram, one is struck

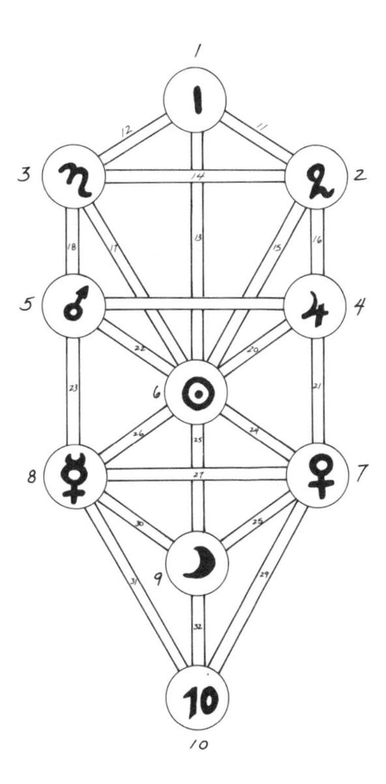

Fig. 42. The Tree of Life

Fig. 43. Sree Yantra

by certain overall resemblances with the outline of the chakra system. Malketh is clearly at the base. Not only is Kether at the crown, but that is what the word "Kether" means. In addition the centers or sephiroths, as they are called, are organized into three groups, upper, middle and lower, in much the same form as used by tantric Buddhist teachings.

Direct parallels have also been drawn between specific sephiroths and chakras. These have been summarized by Dion Fortune[12] in her important work *The Mystical Qabalah* as follows: Malkuth (the sphere of the earth) is associated with the Muladhara

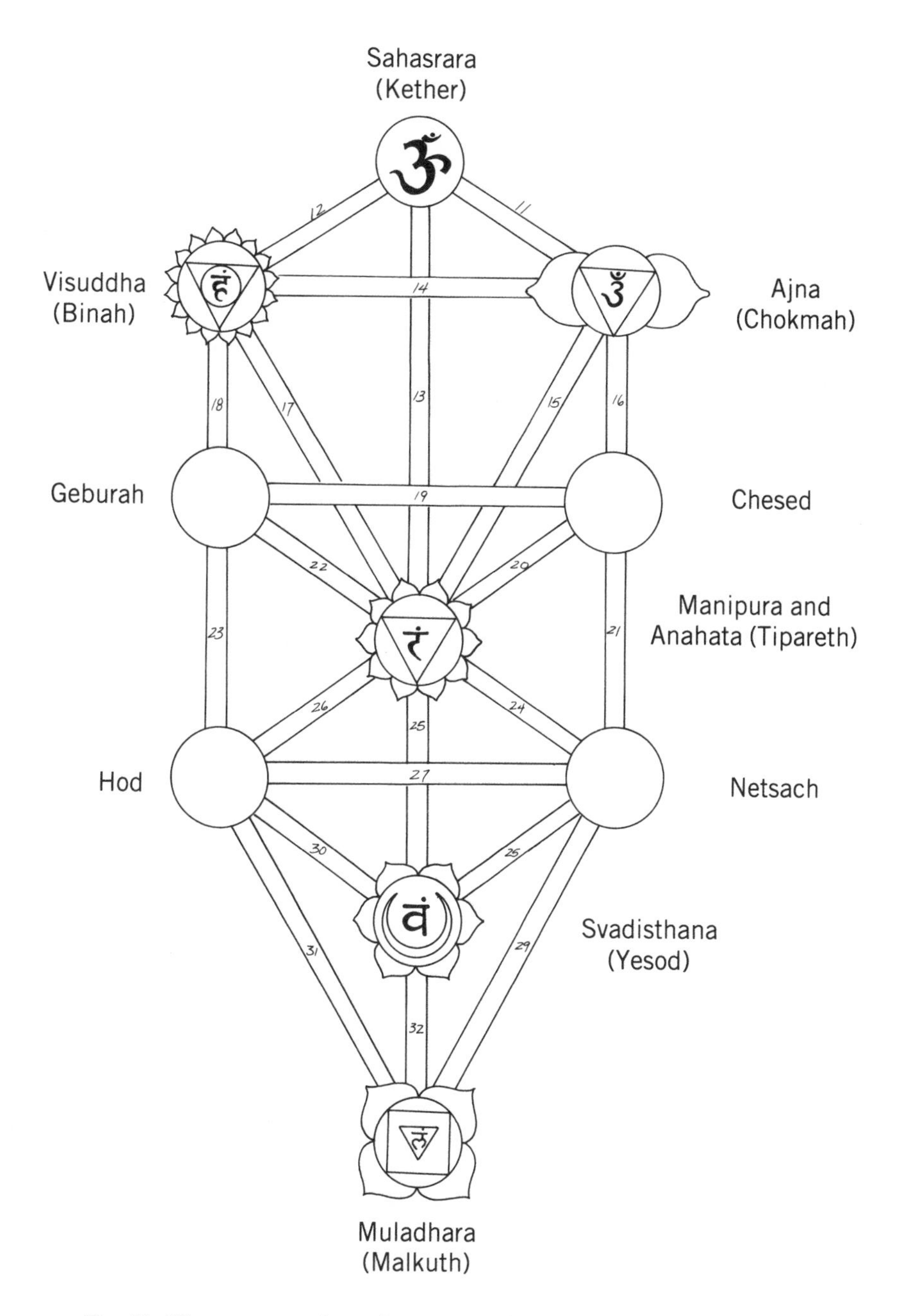

Fig. 44. The correspondence between sephiroths and the chakras

chakra located at the perineum. Yesod is associated with the Svadisthana chakra at the base of the sexual organs. Tiphareth is related to the Manipura and Anahata chakras located in the breast and solar plexus. Binah is associated with the Visuddha chakra in the larynx. Chokma is related to the Ajna chakra at the base of the nose, and Kether is related to the Sahasrara chakra, the thousand-petaled lotus.

Beyond these specific connections, each sephiroth has a variety of associations directly parallel to those noted in the Hindu and Buddhist traditions. Kether, for example, is called the point within the circle or the white head, and is related to union with God or Completion of the Great Work. Chokmah is known as the Illuminating Intelligence, and is associated with the vision of God. Tiphareth is connected with the mystery of the crucifix and the mediating intelligence, both clearly relating to the heart. Yesod is associated with the Vision of the Machinery of the Universe (creation). Malkath, located at the base where Kundalini resides, is variously called the Gate of the Garden of Eden or Malkah the Queen.

It is not only the Sephiroths and their placement that are important, but also the paths connecting the centers to each other, which determine how creation takes place. In this connection it is suggestive that there are 32 such paths. This corresponds exactly with the number of important channels in the subtle body according to the Taoist system. Whether these channels are associated with the symbolism of the paths in the Tree of Life is another question.

In any case, the exploration of the recurrence of the subtle body in different cultural and religious traditions is a task for careful scholarship. It was not our purpose to undertake such a task, but rather to suggest the probability that such a continuity exists. If this has been established then one of our basic goals has been achieved.

CHAPTER SIX

CONCLUSIONS

Having detected an underlying commonality among the different versions of the subtle body that were described in the previous chapters, we must face the endless differences and discrepancies that have arisen in this exploration. There is no problem if the energy body is viewed as a mythological archetype drenched with symbolic meaning. And on one level this is the case. But while it may appear as a dream body or an illusory body in different traditions, the crucial thing about the subtle body is that it is said to exist in the everyday world with as much reality as the physical organism, if it has been activated and developed. If that is so we find ourselves dealing with a kind of spiritual anatomy. And anatomy, at least on the physical level, is pretty much the same for every human being. Therefore if the subtle body exists, how can there be as many contradictory statements about the details of its nature as are presented in the literature on the subject?

Perhaps the most sensible approach to this problem is suggested by the tale of the wise men and the elephant. The wise men were blind. Each of them approached the elephant from a different angle producing an amazing array of conclusions as to the true nature of the elephant.

"He is like a great column," said the first, throwing his arms around one of the elephant's legs, until the elephant in annoyance shoved him away. "And he is very powerful," the wise man added as he picked himself up off the ground.

"No, you are wrong. He is like a rope," said the second wise man pulling on his tail. The elephant did not like this too much either and kicked the man, who said as he staggered to his feet, "He is very, very powerful and must be approached with great care."

"You are wrong," said the third touching the end of his tusk. "He is smooth and comes to a point."

They all proceeded to argue, while standing at a safe distance. Finally the elephant took a great drink of water and sprayed it over his back. Some of the spray happened to fall on a fourth wise man who concluded, "He is very gentle and he falls from the sky."

Needless to say, they were all still arguing as the elephant, who had heard enough of their noise, walked away into the forest.

From the viewpoint of this fable the nearest approximation to the truth would be an integration of all these experiences, but that presupposes a great sampling of the reactions of many persons. However, without such a synthesis one is left trying to visualize something that is like a column, a rope, a spear and a rain shower. The only result is going to be a cosmic headache. But conversely, it doesn't mean that anyone was wrong. They only became wrong when they assumed that their experience was the only possible version of the particular reality.

CONTRADICTIONS IN CHAKRA DESCRIPTIONS

From a more scientific orientation, Neff[1] has recently considered the contradictions in chakra descriptions, ancient and modern, and suggested a number of explanations for these inconsistencies. First, an individual may become confused when experiencing two dimensions simultaneously, the physical and the etheric. Second, the differences in the locations and descriptions of chakras may arise because they are being viewed by different types of psychics. Astral psychics are predisposed to seeing chakras in the front, whereas mental psychics will tune in to the more refined evolutionary energy ascending in the back.

A third explanation is that while there may be many chakras, only those that are most emphasized, and consequently best developed in a given culture, may be described. A clear and fascinating example is found in Durkheim's book *Hara*[2], which describes how Japanese culture is based on the cultivation of the center in the lower belly.

Furthermore, the teacher may see many chakras but talk of only a few for didactic purposes. For example, in Buddhism the upper chakras are often emphasized. The lower ones are not denied, but they are viewed as a less appropriate focus within the Buddhist context.

Then again, a particular tradition may cause one to focus on certain chakras. This is not a cultural limitation, but the particular type of practice within the culture. For example, Christianity, Bhakti Yoga and Sufi mysticism focus primarily on the development of the heart chakra.

Finally, Neff suggests that since chakras are basically experiences of non-physical realms, their physical counterparts are bound to be both variable and approximate.

In addition to these explanations a number of others can be suggested. For example, the subtle body relates to the dream-state level of reality. In tantric Buddhism, subtle body practices and dream-state practices are considered within the same sphere.[3] One of the characteristics of experiences that are near the unconscious realm is that the ordinary laws of logic break down and something can be both "A" and "not A" at the same time. It is the essence of any dream that a person can be himself and someone else. It is only on awakening that these apparent contradictions are united within one's singular world of inner experience. To the extent that subtle body work touches on the area of dreams and mythology, inconsistencies can be expected to occur.

Second, there are political considerations. When a new religion is struggling for life, it seeks to distinguish itself from its rivals. It will not emphasize similarities. Each tradition will go out of its way to create its own symbolic universe.

Third, there is an inevitable tendency to take the experiences of a creative and seminal individual and crystallize them into a ritual practice within the tradition in which they occurred. What started out as a personal event evolves into a formulation required for all. This was never intended, but is very hard to avoid. It is not unusual for teachers themselves to fall victim to the tendency of assuming that their students should experience the same form and sequence of spiritual experience that they have known.

A related assumption also poses a problem; what someone asserts about his own experience is usually true, at least for him. But what he says about the experiences of other traditions is usually false. This occurs because of his own attachment to that which has nourished him, and a corresponding lack of understanding about other traditions.

In the present context it is important to recognize that each approach can and will influence the subtle body in some way, whether the method is direct or not. The Jesus Prayer is a good example. It is presented within an orthodox Christian context of sin and redemption, but its indirect effect is to open the throat and heart chakras.

Many other examples could be given. Cultivation of love and compassion in Bhakti Yoga, Christianity and Mahayana Buddhism must inevitably develop the heart center. Practice of martial arts encourages centering in the lower belly, whether it is specifically taught or not. Any systematic spiritual practice that has stood the test of time is likely to have some effect on the subtle body, which is usually detectible if you search for it. Saint Therese of Lisieux, for example, experienced a period of fits, hallucinations and strange, spontaneous acrobatics totally unrelated to Christian practice, but quite understandable in the context of kundalini yoga.

The more direct approach that consciously seeks to cultivate the chakras may seem the most sensible, but it is not necessarily the most effective for all people in every situation. It does, however, have the virtue of clarity within its own sphere, and the results that it produces may be easier to accept if one has consciously set out to attain them.

If one looks at any approach that has successfully endured for a significantly long period of time, one sees an amalgam of tradition, belief, cultural influence, the particular inner experience of its originator and, finally, a practical method. It is difficult, if not impossible, to separate the various impacts of these diverse influences, particularly when they become drenched with the belief that is inherent in many practices. To a Buddhist, all Buddhist methods are the best. But if one focuses on the practical element—what you actually do—it is possible to discover strategies used by some traditions that are also used by a number of other traditions and which seem, on one level, to be testable outside the context in which they occur.

THE THREE BODY MODEL

Before examining such strategies in greater detail, it is helpful to classify a variety of different traditions in order to clarify their basic nature. Perhaps the simplest model is based on the three body concept which uses awareness, energy and qualities as its fundamental dimensions. This scheme roughly parallels the physical, subtle and cosmic bodies. While most methods offer varied combinations of these three dimensions, some are sufficiently weighted in a particular direction to clarify the model.

For example, in Hinayana Buddhism, in certain aspects of Zen Buddhism and in the teachings of such modern masters as Krishnamurti and Maharshi, almost exclusive attention is placed on the cultivation of awareness.

Emphasis on energy flow and transformation is found in many forms of yoga. In general, the previous chapters have documented this form of practice.

Methods that focus on positive universal qualities which simply exist, in contrast to energy that flows from one place to another, are found in many traditional religions. Frequently called "good works," they may be combined with prayer as means of character development. In advanced mystical practices such as the formless paths in tantric Buddhism (including Mahamudra, Ati Yoga and the Yoga of Great Liberation) almost exclusive emphasis is placed on higher states of consciousness and being.

If the three-part distinction of our three-body model is valid, it should be possible to classify any approach in terms of the relative weight of the three elements involved; awareness, energy flow and higher qualities. This classification should then allow us to form some basis of comparison. This exercise could be quite useful because the endless differences in detail may prove to be more apparent than real.

IDENTIFYING UNDERLYING STRATEGIES

As a further development, one could focus on testing the strategies that are employed in a particular system. Testing strategies could be described as a typically American approach to mysticism; find out what works and use it. In this case, determining what works is difficult because each method is deeply embedded in its own historical and cultural context. But it is not difficult to isolate recurrent principles and strategies in the methods that have endured. This may not prove the validity of the strategies, but it will help to clarify whether or not they are worth investigating.

A number of examples can be given to illustrate the possibilities of this approach.

1. Focus the mind. Any method that requires a particular picture, image or thought to be maintained utilizes this strategy. It is so widely employed that the principle is usually taken for granted, whether it occurs as part of a prayer, an awareness exercise, or in visualizing a deity.

2. The more modalities, the better. This approach is best illustrated by the tantric tradition where all sensory, emotional and attitudinal components are woven together within the ritual practice. The opposite alternative is also an important strategy, namely "eliminate everything." This is the underlying strategy of classical ascetic practice. Everything that is desirable should be sacrificed.

3. Reduce everything to a point. In this strategy every experience is returned to its point of origin. Nothing remains but the void from which the point itself emerged. The mandala is a clear example of a sacred diagram in which the total experience is generated from the bindu point in the center. If one can reverse this flow and return all manifestation to a point, one has temporary freedom. When it re-manifests, it is a fresh experience.

4. Distinguish between the way things are and how they may be transformed. This principle is basic to all alchemical operations. Simply noting properties is a purely descriptive undertaking. Utilizing the potentials of these properties opens up new possibilities, whether in organic chemistry or in the energies of the subtle body. On the whole, Hinduism has emphasized the descriptive, whereas tantric Buddhism has focused on transformative potential. Thus the Hindu might ask what element is associated with a particular chakra, whereas a Buddhist would be more likely to investigate the result of bringing another element into the same chakra.

5. Look for parallels that are usually ignored. This is the strategy of inter-system investigation. For example, Buddhists speak of bindus, whereas Taoists talk of crystals. Comparative analysis suggests that they are the same thing—condensed higher energies. Furthermore, there are 64 wisdom dakinis of transformation in the belly in both tantric Hinduism and Buddhism and 64 symbols in the I Ching system of divination. Finally, practices such as self-intercourse in Taoism and the four blisses in Mahamudra Buddhism both involve an element of internal fulfillment, although their objectives are not the same.

6. Build up great pressure and then provide a sudden release. This principle was employed by John the Baptist, who immersed the person to be baptized until they truly needed air. When they were released and pronounced saved, there was a great physiological shift as they were able to breathe again, which greatly intensified the overall experience. Meditation on Zen koans utilizes the same principle.

7. Identify with a higher being. This principle is implicitly or explicitly woven into most religious practices. One might say that the underlying purpose of spiritual work is to establish a contact between the individual and a being of a higher nature. Through this contact the individual is either gradually or abruptly altered. The Catholic mass employs this strategy, as does shamanism, or indeed membership in any religious community. Without the utilization of this principle one could say that there is no religion.

8. Temporarily become a higher being yourself. In some traditions this approach might be viewed as sacrilegious. In others it is seen as quite natural. The Tibetan oracle clearly sets out to temporarily become a deity in order to be able to predict the future, as did the priests and priestesses of various pagan cults. Saints often achieve an identity with a higher religious manifestation that may be demonstrated through such phenomena as stigmata. In the East, many traditions consciously set out to attract and visualize the deity as a living entity so that the devotee may merge with it and, in this way, obtain its particular qualities and powers.

9. Utilize all three bodies in the practice. This would involve a form of spiritual development that combined awareness, conscious energy flow and higher qualities of being. An interesting example of such a practice is "fusion," a Taoist practice described in detail in Part II.

10. Create your ideal self. This strategy is similar to identifying with a deity but, in this case, one focuses on a perfect version of oneself. No religious belief is required. By continuous visualization the ideal self begins to take on a life of its own. This is a typically Taoist alternative to focusing on a deity.

11. Act the way you would like to become or become the way you would like to act. The first alternative is typically Western. If you act as if you are confident, you will become so. The second alternative is typically Eastern. If you imagine you are a lion (which is by nature confident), then the confidence will be there effortlessly. Both approaches are valid and employed in varying degrees by different methods. And most important from the viewpoint of the practitioner, if one approach doesn't work, the other may.

12. Discover how different traditions complement each other. As with the blind men and the elephant, different approaches may fit together to provide a more complete picture than any of them supplies by itself. This principle is particularly difficult to apply because followers are blinded by their own commitments to their particular practices. However, it is possible and always fascinating when a missing piece can be put into place.

For example, dumo breathing in tantric Buddhism is usually described in terms of taking air into the belly and rotating the belly to mix the various energies. If this process is combined with the Taoist iron shirt practice of "packing"[4], the effect is greatly enhanced. But this particular combination does not occur in either tradition. It has to be discovered by experimentation, which always runs the risk of contaminating the basic practices involved.

13. Expand a negative experience into infinity and it will disappear. A simple example of this practice is focus on personal anger and let it expand until it fills the whole universe. In the process it will change from an immediate destructive reaction into a universal phenomenon in which the original cause is swallowed up. It is possible to do this with all negative experience, neutralizing the negative energy in the process.

14. Utilize configurations. This is the principle underlying all sacred architectural symbols and designs. It is so fundamental that it is easy to ignore. Whatever one is doing can be enhanced by arranging the spatial elements so that they produce the maximum impact. This can be seen in the design of a church or a theater. It is always possible to arrive at a spatial arrangement in which the resonance of the phenomena it contains is greatly enhanced.

15. Following tradition versus acting spontaneously. Usually tradition is followed closely in the early and middle stages of practice. It is only in the more advanced levels, after a basic foundation has been established, that spontaneity and the free inner evolvement of experience is emphasized, a tendency that is seen with particular clarity in Tibetan Buddhism.

16. View the chakra as a universe in itself. This orientation is clearly seen in the Hindu and Buddhist approaches toward the chakras. Realizing that each chakra is like a separate entity allows one to approach it with greater awareness and sensitivity, and to appreciate the universal aspect that it expresses in its microcosmic form.

17. All energy flow is either in a straight line, a circle, a spiral, or radiates outward from a point. There may be a few exceptions, but this single sentence seems to cover the basic possibilities and can be used to suggest new alternatives as the individual explores the subtle body practices with which he is most familiar. Thus, an exercise might focus on drawing energy from one chakra to another in a straight line. A chakra itself could be moved in a circle, that is, it could revolve; or the energy could spiral instead of moving in a straight line, gathering momentum in the process. Finally, as in a mandala, the energy can radiate from a point in all directions. In this case the point represents the interface between energy body dynamics and the space body qualities that manifest everywhere simultaneously.

Many other examples of mystical strategies could be given, but these are sufficient to illustrate the possibilities of the approach.

ALCHEMY - EAST AND WEST

On a more global level of analysis the subtle body cannot be fully understood without placing it in the context of Eastern and Western alchemy. In Hinduism the concept of inner transformation through the utilization of three or more bodies encompasses the detailed description of subtle body processes. It is not always clear whether these bodies are born with the individual or not, but their necessity for different phases of spiritual development is evident.

Furthermore, the basic concept of kundalini yoga as a process of progressive refinement of natural energy manifestations represents a kind of alchemical process. In this process each stage leads organically to the next, until they culminate in the lotus chakra where the feminine creative energy of kundalini and the masculine energy of Shiva finally come together and create a stepping stone for all higher levels of manifestation.

Differences between Buddhist and Hindu alchemy are of importance to practitioners of each approach, but often hard to appreciate from the outside. Much of the relevant material in Buddhist tantra has recently become more accessible in such works as *Clear Light of Bliss*.[5] The sequential nature of higher development is carefully developed as a series of purifications and transformations of existing energies and inner structures.

In Taoism, beyond the introductory purification and intermediate energy channel work, the basic purpose is to perform a type of alchemy that will create a soul, that in turn can act as a "baby-sitter" for the final creation of the spirit body. In Taoist alchemy the higher bodies do not initially exist. They must be formed through a kind of internal intercourse. While the creation may take just a moment, like the fertilization of a human egg, the process of maturing the new organism is a matter of decades. Unlike human maturation, this growth of higher bodies can only happen through conscious intent and continuing awareness. The Taoists seem to have used the biological process of reproduction as a precise analogy for the mystical development of soul and spirit.

Some sense of the peculiar mixture of the everyday and the mysterious that characterizes the Taoist approach can be found in Charles Luk's *Taoist Yoga*[6]. It contains a great deal of information about the transformative aspects of Taoist practice, but still only scratches the surface of what is available in the almost 1,200 Taoist classics that have yet to be translated.

In comparison to Hindu and Buddhist tantra, Taoist yoga's approach is sometimes simpler and more archaic. Emphasis is not on compassion for all beings or identifying with pantheons of deities, though they certainly have their place in the Taoist religion. Rather the Tao is the immanent creative principle in the

Fig. 45. Alchemical union

Fig. 45. Alchemical union (cont.)

universe that cannot be named, but can only be approached by the transformation and balancing of the forces within the individual. The Taoist seeks to create an immortal body, which can serve as a vehicle for his manifestation anywhere in the known and unknown universe. This is, in a sense, a highly individualistic approach that seeks not to obliterate the ordinary self, but to transform and expand it beyond known limits in an endless process of self-development.

Alchemy also has a long, although somewhat tarnished tradition in the West. In its outer aspects it constituted a pre-chemical and semi-magical attempt to turn base metals, such as lead, into

Fig. 45. Alchemical union (cont.)

gold; something that until the development of the atomic age we could not really do.

In medieval times of strong religious belief and equally strong punishments for heresy, the alchemist used his laboratory as a protected setting for the creation of a model of an inner process of transformation similar to the intent of his companions in the East engaged in spiritual alchemy. Base metals represented natural energy such as found in the base chakra. Gold was the final result of the inner transformation process and was portrayed literally in the shining auras of holy figures. This process could only be successfully undertaken with endless patience. It was sometimes portrayed in a series of drawings. In his exploration of the psychological aspects of alchemy, Jung[7] presents examples of such pictures. While each has its unique features the underlying process is similar. In one series a couple is shown facing each other holding hands; their clothing disappears; symbols appear in their hands; they sit together in a bath (the cauldron of transformation); they lie down together, and literally become one body as a child emerges from the bath and disappears into the clouds; they wait, not being able to revert to their original separate condition; finally the child reappears. In the last picture a two-headed being emerges as a new creation standing on the moon, surrounded by the tree of life, serpents and a bird.

It is clear that a Western tantric approach is indicated, a blending of masculine and feminine giving rise to a new being. The alchemy occurs in a cauldron in what is essentially an energy process. While the emphasis is not on the chakras as such, it is apparent that the new bodies that are created are on the level of the energy and space bodies.

CONCLUSIONS

All of the preceding suggests several fundamental conclusions which can be summarized in a few sentences. Advanced spiritual development depends on the cultivation of higher bodies. The subtle body provides the vital intervening link in this process. Whether it is made explicit or not, the inner evolution of the individual lies at the core of religious and mystical experience. In this context the subtle body is not an idle curiosity, but represents a critical step in the spiritual process.

Part II

Awakening The Subtle Body

Awakening the Subtle Body

The purpose of Part II is to provide the reader with practical exercises that can be used to awaken and cultivate the subtle body. These methods will allow one to test the reality of the material presented in Part I through direct experience.

Under traditional circumstances a person would contact methods for working on the subtle body in the context of a particular teaching. Such an approach introduces a number of other factors to the experience; the personality of the teacher, his particular training, the attitude of his students, the need for faith and so on. For better or worse you do not have to be concerned with these factors here.

On the other hand, a vital element in any teaching is the act of transmission; receiving the teaching from someone who has already mastered it and has the effects of the teaching functioning within him. When this occurs, not only an understanding of the method is provided, but also a special quality of energy that acts like a cosmic fertilizer on the seed that the teacher plants. While the authors of this book are presenting material with which they are thoroughly familiar, there is no way that a transmission from teacher to student can be fully achieved through the mass media.

At a later point this might become a real issue. But we do not think it need concern you now. The methods to be presented can be practiced by anyone interested in trying them, and if faithfully pursued can produce a useful result. That is sufficient! When this result has been achieved there will be ample opportunity to decide which teacher or teaching you might choose to pursue should you wish to do so.

How you proceed at this point is up to you. While you may only feel a casual interest, the choice is a serious one. You are dealing with a vital intervening link in your own development. There may be many approaches that can be followed, but the reality of the subtle body and its place in the development of any form of inner alchemy cannot be ignored, any more than you can digest food without a stomach.

The more you can relate your own wishes and needs to your present situation, the greater your motivation will become. While a purely experimental attitude is perfectly acceptable, (and in some ways it is ideal), it is also necessary to care about your own potential and the process of its unfolding. Otherwise, why bother to test anything? The best way to start, therefore, is to find something in yourself that really wants to know, experience and develop. It exists, or you wouldn't be reading this book, but most of the time it is off-stage. The moment has come when you will need it, because the energy that it contains will help to produce a partial transmission between you and the exercises.

The situation is similar to an actor rehearsing his lines, while the director continually interrupts demanding, "do it again, with more feeling," until both actor and director really believe what the actor is saying. In this case you are the audience, the actor and the director. And the decision involved is completely up to you. Blind faith in any of these methods is not required; you just have to be open, curious and have a real need to attain a deeper understanding of your own nature.

These methods have been selected from various traditions, ancient and modern. They have been tested by the authors and found to be effective. It is in keeping with the spirit of this book to have picked a broad range of practices in order to expose the reader to many alternative approaches. In each case an effort has been made to: describe how the method is to be performed in a step by step manner, utilizing diagrams where helpful; discuss where and when it is appropriate to do them and what they are intended to accomplish; identify special difficulties that might occur; and examine specific strategies underlying the methods being presented. Utilizing this multidimensional approach, the reader can learn not only how to perform the practice but also to understand why and how they are doing it. The methods are classified in terms of their underlying objectives; purification of the subtle body, opening the chakras, strengthening the energy flow and the use of interpersonal influences. The practices are also arranged in three levels of difficulty. Be humble! Start at the elementary level no matter what your previous experience may be. Don't go on to the next level until you are sure that you are obtaining a useful result on the previous one. Your own experience will have to be your guide. It will tell you what you need to know and gradually enable you to begin to sense the reality and significance of the subtle body in your own inner development. Then, and only then, can you begin to decide what path you should follow over the longer term of your conscious evolvement.

Fig. 46. The inner smile

INTRODUCTORY EXERCISES

PURIFICATION
The Inner Smile

This purification exercise is taken from Taoist sources[1]. It is extremely simple but its effect is instantaneous if it is done properly. As with any purification process it can be undertaken either as a means of preparing for a period of inner work or as the need arises during the day. It does not require special conditions and can be utilized outside of any Taoist context. There are no particular cautions or difficulties associated with the practice. It is rather a question of how much time and effort you wish to put into it. Obviously the effect will vary with the time invested, but not necessarily in direct proportion. If done in the midst of an intense everyday event for even a minute, it can alter one's inner state for the better in a startling manner.

The exercise is based on the positive energy that people express when they smile spontaneously. Starting from the experience of such a smile, which may be stimulated by an appropriate memory, looking at something you enjoy, or just smiling because you feel good, you focus on the energy associated with the smile. This is a happy, healing energy. The basic purpose of this exercise is to generate, identify with and then spread this energy throughout the body. If this is accomplished the happy energy drives out the sad, and relaxation eliminates tension.

A typical pattern of extending the smile experience might be as follows:

1. Identify the energy through a spontaneous smile.

2. Extend the energy to the left eye; the right eye.

3. The left ear; the right ear.

4. The tongue.

5. The voice box.

6. The left lung; the right lung.

7. The heart.

8. The whole body feeling and expressing the inner smile.

Do each step slowly. There is no time limit. Don't shift to the next step until you really feel the smiling energy in the previous one. The more relaxed you are to begin with, the easier the process will be. But the less relaxed you are the more you need the exercise. So don't be discouraged if the experience eludes you in a disturbed moment.

The eventual purpose is to feel your whole body smiling, every organ, bone, nerve and cell. This can best be approached through small specific steps. A variety of different sequences is possible. You can smile in different bones, nerves, blood vessels, glands, different structural parts (for example, each joint in each finger, one at a time). But however you approach it, the inner smile will make the particular part feel better immediately as you substitute a positive healing energy for the numbness and negativity that may have been there without your having even been aware of it.

A traditional Taoist sequence for practicing the inner smile is as follows:

Forehead, nose, cheeks, mouth, neck, throat, thymus, heart, lungs, liver, kidneys, pancreas, spleen, lower abdomen, genitals and finally the eyes. The process should unfold as a flow of sensation from one area to the next, rather then a series of mechanical shifts. It should feel natural.

The basic strategy that is involved in this approach is to focus your attention on a positive energy. Then by systematically shifting your attention you can spread the energy, as if you had touched a lighted match to different places in a pile of dry kindling.

When you have had a clear experience with spreading energy in this way you may be left wondering why everyone doesn't do it all the time. It is as if we don't really want to feel good. Either we don't like ourselves enough or it takes too much effort.

OPENING CHAKRAS

Attention and Conscious Breathing[2]

In the average person the chakras are closed. It takes exceptional circumstances or unusual effort to open them, even though the experience feels quite natural when it occurs. The following exercise is designed to initiate the opening process. It consists of two distinct parts that fit together organically after each has been developed separately.

The first stage involves the focusing of attention, a process that is greatly emphasized in Hinayana Buddhism. Perhaps the fundamental freedom that anyone possesses is the choice of where to put their attention. Whether it is placed internally on a sensation or externally on a perception, or in an imaginary place that does not really exist, the effect of focusing awareness is to attract energy to that spot.

A chakra is like a bud. It requires energy in order to open. Attention can be employed as a means of drawing the energy to the required spot. In the present context, if attention is placed at the site of a chakra and held there in a focused and relaxed manner for 30 to 60 seconds, the chakra may begin to stir.

As a preliminary experiment, try the following. Locate the approximate position of the Ajna chakra (the third eye). It is about two fingers-widths above the bridge of the nose. Touch the spot with your index finger as a means of beginning to attract your attention to that area. Then for 30 seconds focus your awareness there. Do not let anything distract you, but at the same time stay quiet. Pause and observe any effect that has occurred. Has the sensation changed in the area? Do you feel a throb, itch, warmth, trembling, or has nothing happened at all? Don't try to anticipate the experience in advance. You can't really know what you are going to feel. Just accept whatever sensation occurs without exaggeration or neglect. If you feel anything at all, try the experiment again for another 30 seconds. After that, how does it feel? Don't expect anything incredible. When a bud begins to open, it is a subtle experience.

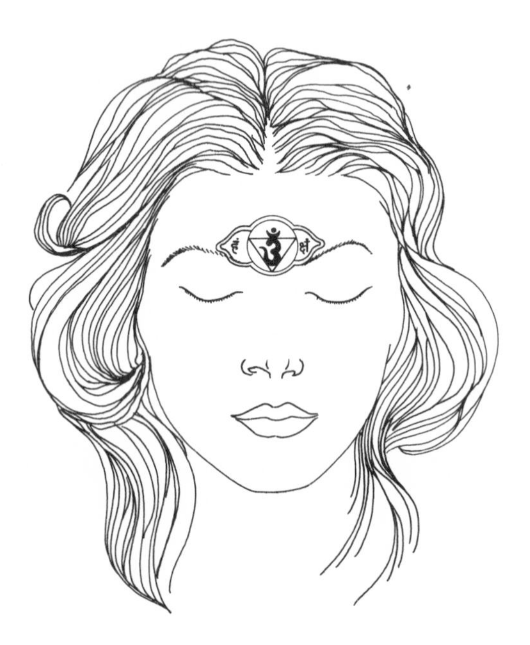

Fig. 47. Ajna chakra

It is usually more effective to work for a brief, concentrated period, observe the effect, and then repeat the process. If that meets with any success, then the process can be extended for five minutes. Attention is a tool. It attracts energy where it is needed and increases your awareness of the sensation in the area at the same time. Furthermore, the more you can relax, the greater will be the amount of free energy that can be attracted to the site of your awareness. But whatever your experience, the basic purpose is to direct energy to the chakra bud so that it can begin to stir and eventually unfurl, petal by petal.

The second part of this approach can be called "conscious breathing". It is related to pranayama yoga, but unlike the specific artificial patterns of breathing that characterize those yogic methods, it might be considered generic breathing that integrates sensation, emotion and understanding in a conscious action in order to intensify and expand the amount of energy that can be extracted from the surrounding atmosphere.

Begin by breathing in through your nose as if you were smelling a rose; with enjoyment, awareness and understanding of your wish and need to absorb the energy that the rose's odor and the air contains. Hold your breath as if you were savoring the bouquet of fine wine, relaxing and letting the sensation spread through your body. Then release your breath while at the same time surrendering negative emotions and tensions so that they are free to flow out of the body with the breath. Pause until the physiological and psychological need to start the cycle again begins to assert itself. Try it a few times until the whole process begins to feel natural.

This form of conscious breathing can be used as an energizing and purification process, each complete breathing cycle producing a definite step toward a better inner condition. It can also be combined with the focusing of attention on the chakra bud,

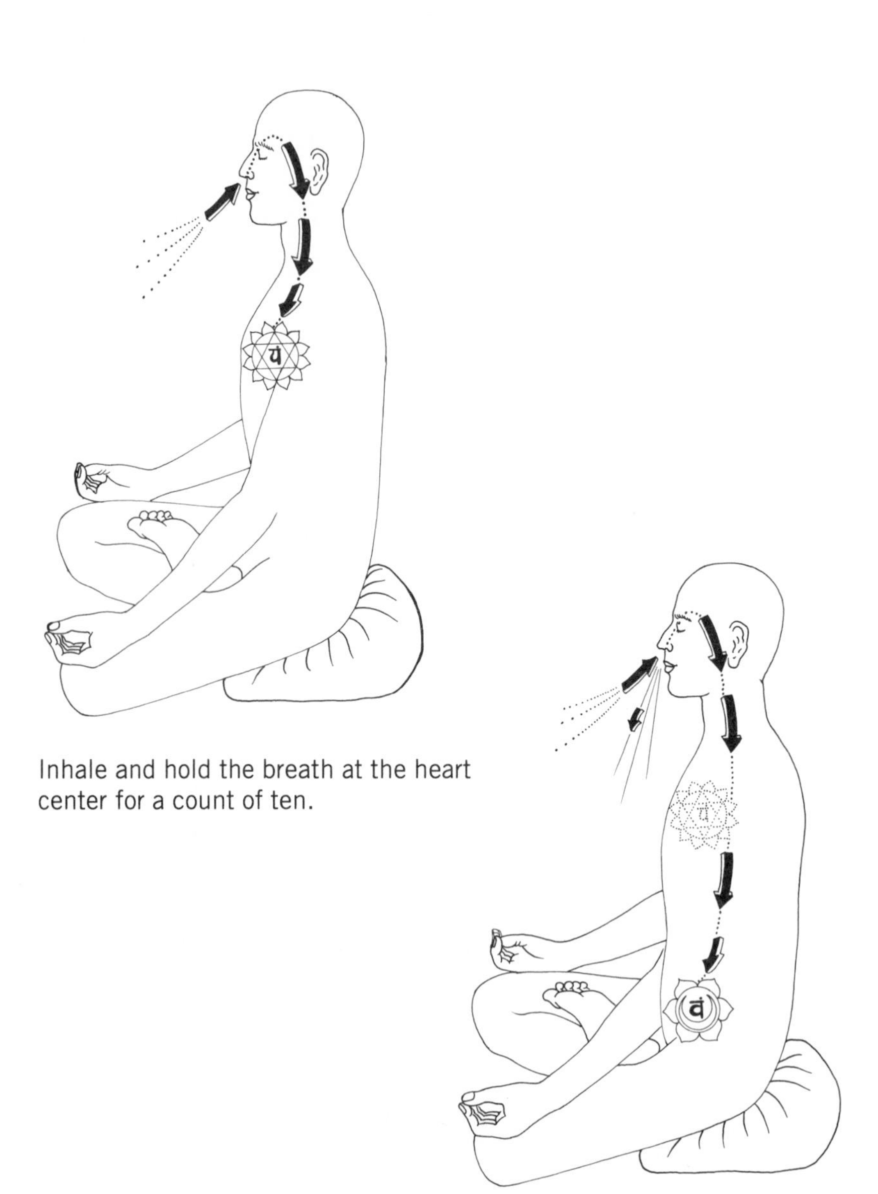

Fig. 48. The double breath

producing an intensification of the process. Once each procedure is clear, you can begin to experiment with combining them.

First, focus on the area to which energy is to be drawn, using the third eye as the point of departure. Having established a clear focus, begin the conscious breathing. Most of the energy that is drawn in with the breath will go where your attention is focused. As you hold your breath and relax, the energy will have a chance to expand and penetrate deeper. When you let go of your breath, various obstacles and resistances can flow out, allowing the energy greater freedom to operate. After a few cycles of breathing, pause, note the effect, and then start again.

There is no danger in this process. The most important thing is to be conscious of each step that you take, and to remember what you are trying to attain—the opening of the chakra.

CIRCULATING THE FLOW

The Double Breath[3]

This exercise resembles Dumo breathing in Tibetan Buddhism, but it is the discovery of an American yogi, Swami Rudrananda. Its purpose is to establish a flow down the center line of the body with particular emphasis on the functioning of the heart and navel chakras. This exercise follows very naturally from the previous one. If the use of attention and conscious breathing has begun to open a chakra, the double breath will naturally intensify the process.

The basic function of the double breath is to produce a supercharging action that is created by piling one breath cycle on top of the next. It has been described as follows:

> One draws in the breath high up through the nose and into the heart center. As one starts the breath into the heart, one

> swallows in the throat and tries to feel the energy travel down to the heart center. The swallow is to release tension in the throat chakra and allow energy to expand there. After swallowing, one continues to inhale breath in the heart center until the lungs are filled to their maximum capacity. The breath is held in the heart chakra for about the count of ten. The time count may become longer as strength is gained in the breathing. During the time when the breath is held, one must try and sense deeply within the heart center and, from the very core of one's being, ask to surrender to, and receive, the cosmic energy (in the atmosphere). After the breath has been held for the count of ten, one exhales one-fifth of the air and inhales again, bringing the energy and the concentration to the chakra just below the navel. The breath is retained in the navel chakra for about the count of ten and then exhaled very slowly. This double breathing may be repeated ... about every three minutes.

Go through the description slowly, as often as is necessary to begin to get an organic sense of what is involved. There is no hurry. The sequence of actions may be somewhat confusing at first, particularly at the moment when the attention shifts to the lower belly. What is required is a syncopated action. One shifts attention to the lower belly slightly before letting out of one-fifth of the air. There is nothing intrinsically difficult about it. The more relaxed that you are, the easier the exercise will be and the greater its effect.

INTERPERSONAL ASPECTS

The Flow In Others

To the extent that we are open to their influence, the people that we meet affect our inner state. These spontaneous influences can be tapped to help us open our chakras. When we meet someone in whom a particular quality is very open or strong, it will affect us in the same area. If another person has an open heart, it will help our heart to open.

The basic exercise is simple. When another person energizes one of our chakras we must first of all be aware that it is happening, and secondly utilize the opportunity to focus on the appropriate area and draw the energy that we take in as we breathe into the chakra, somewhat like blowing on hot coals. In a sense, the other person does the work. We only have to be aware of what is happening and make the effort to enhance it.

The basic strategy that is employed in this exercise is similar to the hidden tantric method[4] used by nuns and priests who have taken an oath of celibacy. They utilize this approach to allow another individual to stimulate their heart or sex chakra from a distance. By being aware of the effect and working with it, they are able to use others to intensify their own inner flow while remaining true to their vows.

This approach is quite simple, but also profound. Usually we are caught by the impact of others and our energy flows to them. But this method allows us to reverse the flow and build on the impact that others have on us to open something in ourselves.

INTERMEDIATE EXERCISES

PURIFICATION

Vajrasattva Cleansing[5]

This ritual is a typical example of a multidimensional tantric approach. Its basic purpose is to purge all regrettable and evil actions. It is associated with Vajrasattva, the tantric deity who has the power to remove all difficulties and disturbances.

Each step will be described separately, but the actual process should flow naturally from one stage to another when the practitioner is familiar with the process.

1. Be seated comfortably.
2. Visualize Vajrasattva seated above your head. Within his heart center is the sacred syllable "HUM." Be aware of the joy and purity that he expresses and experiences.
3. Recite the sacred mantra "Om Vajrasattva Hum" 108 times.
4. At the end of this time allow ambrosia to begin to flow from the "HUM" in Vajrasattva's heart onto the top of your head. As it is absorbed in the crown of the head, all of the psychic poisons, sins and illnesses stored in the cells of the body begin to be released and flow toward the ground.
5. Below the earth are various hungry monsters and demons. They rise up out of the earth to consume the poisons that the body is releasing, because these poisons are their natural food.
6. As the body is purified, the ambrosia flowing into your head spreads through the chakras filling, in turn, the third eye, the throat, heart center, navel, sex and base of spine centers with beauty and bliss.

Fig. 49. Visualizing Vajrasattva seated above the head.

7. Ask Vajrasattva to forgive you for all your past sins, using your own words to make the request.
8. Hopefully Vajrasattva smiles and forgives you using his own words.
9. Vajrasattva turns into light and merges with you. You become Vajrasattva!
10. Your body begins to shrink, smaller and smaller, until it turns into a point of light in the heart center which finally disappears into emptiness, like a spark going out. This concludes the exercise.

There are a number of extensions and variations of this ritual for the more experienced practitioner, but the foregoing gives the basic process.

The first time that you attempt to perform this purification, set aside a half hour so that you can proceed in a relaxed manner. Be clear about each step before you go on to the next. As the process becomes more familiar, it can be done in five to ten minutes, after which you can pass on to the other chakra exercises.

A purification is both useful in itself, and is also a natural prelude to working with any of the chakras. The purer you are inside, the easier it is to obtain results. If you begin in an angry, frustrated or clogged condition, the entire time that you devote to inner practice may be used in just getting to a more balanced place from which to start.

This ritual illustrates a number of the principles associated with tantric Buddhist practice. First, the use of a deity associated with the function to be cultivated is highly characteristic. It humanizes the action and puts it into the context of a dialogue with a higher power whose help is sought. Second is the use of sacred syllables, phrases and numbers to energize the process. Third is the extensive use of visualization; of the deity, the ambrosia, the demons and so on. Fourth is the filling of the purified chakras with ambrosia as the final step in their revitalization. Fifth is the interchange with the deity in which you ask for and hopefully receive forgiveness. Sixth is becoming one with the deity, which completes the purification process on the cellular level. And finally, seventh is disappearing into the void from which all manifestations arise. In this way the practitioner avoids the risk of blowing up his ego with the idea that he is the same as the deity, which would only create something else needing purification in the future.

OPENING CHAKRAS

Prayer and Imagination[6]

Almost every tradition uses some form of imagination and prayer. These two processes are distinct, like breathing and focusing, but they complement each other. By "prayer" we mean asking a higher power for help. Imagination is a visual expression of the "as if" principle. If you can imagine it happening, then it is possible that it could happen. Putting the two together produces the following sequence. First, you ask for help. Next you imagine a positive outcome as vividly as possible. And then, hopefully, it happens. For purposes of illustration we will focus on opening the navel chakra, though any of the chakras could be used, as follows:

1. In order to pray, the heart center must be open, because the prayer must come from the heart if it is to be effective. Therefore, spend a few minutes working on the heart center using the first half of the double breath. When you feel the beginning of a response, proceed.
2. Let your prayer issue from the heart center. This is a very distinct and probably unfamiliar experience. It feels as if a

Fig. 50. The flowering of the navel center.

little voice is speaking from the upper center of your chest. Using your own words, ask for help in opening your navel chakra. It doesn't matter whether you are asking a higher power or your own higher self. It is the sincerity of the asking that counts. Listen to your voice. Does it sound as if you mean it? If it doesn't, ask again. Work to open your heart a little more. After you have asked, do nothing—just wait. See what happens. You can't make it happen. The whole point of the prayer is to put the matter into someone else's hands. All you can do is surrender.

Probably you will be surprised to find that when you ask sincerely with a voice from the heart center, there is a response without any further effort on your part.

3. Having performed the preceding, you are ready to begin the visualization. Close your eyes. Feel the navel chakra as a large bud buried in your lower stomach two finger widths below your belly button. From somewhere high above and in front of you visualize a clear beam of light that shines on the bud, like light coming through a break in the clouds. After you see the light, try to feel the warmth that it brings to your lower belly. Once the image is clear, experience the opening of the bud, petal by petal, like time-lapse photography. Any accompanying sensation should be noted and amplified because it means that the experience is passing from the realm of a guided daydream to an actual inner event. These sensations might include stretching, trembling, warmth, pain, or a feeling of radiance. They are different for each person and different at different times for the same person. They constitute the physiological aspect of the opening of the chakra. Keep coming back to the living light beam. Slowly watch the navel chakra open like a great chrysanthemum that can extend beyond the limits of your body.

When the process seems complete, do several double breaths. Ask again for help in opening the chakra. And then relax!

The major strategies that are employed in the process are: involving a higher power in attaining what you are trying to achieve by asking it for help; surrendering after you have asked so as to allow the opportunity for a response to occur; and imagining that you are attaining the desired result by utilizing an appropriate image, for example, light on the bud.

CIRCULATION
The Ha Rite

This exercise involves the exchange and circulation of energies and is based on the Ha Rite of the Kahuna Polynesians[7]. They view this rite as a type of energized prayer that utilizes the three selves that they believe make up the individual. These selves are roughly similar to the three bodies of the Hindu, Buddhist and Taoist traditions. The lower self is related to the physical body. The middle self is everyday conscious awareness, which is roughly comparable to the subtle body. The higher self is parallel to the cosmic body. In a relatively simple manner the Ha Rite organizes and integrates all three selves in the prayer experience.

In the previous exercise prayer was used to obtain help in opening a chakra, so it was not necessary to consider any of the more general problems that may occur when you make a wish, as you do when you pray. There are two major difficulties. First, you may not get what you ask for, which could be frustrating and disillusioning. Second, the prayer may be granted, in which case you will discover the hard way whether you made a wise wish or not. Judging by fairy tales, people often wish for things they later have to undo. Thus, even if you are skeptical, you should pick your wish with care. It is usually safe to ask for whatever may help your growth. If still in doubt you can always end with the phrase, "Grant me this prayer only if it will help my own development and not hurt others in the process."

There are four steps in the Ha Rite:

1. Take four slow, deep breaths. Let your middle conscious self (everyday awareness), command your lower self to gather the higher energy in the atmosphere as you breathe and pack it into your stomach.
2. Ask your lower self to send out a call to the higher self to establish contact between them.
3. Let the middle self recall its prayer and feel as if it is already answered. It should also feel that enough energy has been accumulated in the stomach to be able to proceed and that all three selves are connected by the faith that it has in the outcome.
4. The higher energy that has been accumulated in the belly is allowed to flow upward into the space above the head where the higher self resides. At the same time prayer is expressed in words, and the result that is sought is seen as vividly as possible. Having done all of this, the final result is given to the safekeeping of the higher self.

This exercise is an appropriate way to conclude a meditation period. To the extent that the inner flow has already been established, the Ha Rite will be easier to perform and it will help to integrate the period of inner work that it concludes.

There are a number of interesting strategies employed in this form of prayer: the need to establish communication between the various selves in order to obtain the desired result; the need to accumulate additional energy in order to activate the prayer process; the recognition of the hierarchical relation of the different selves (which is most clearly expressed by offering up the accumulated energy gathered by the lower and middle selves to the higher self along with the prayer); surrendering everything once the effort has been made; letting each self function in a way that is natural to it.

INTERPERSONAL ASPECTS

Working With Religious Art[8]

It is possible to use works of art as a source of nourishment for the subtle body. Religious art, in particular, is created with this possibility in mind. If one concentrates on a sacred image, one can open to the energy that it transmits. Whether it is a photograph, statue or painting, the fact that it portrays a higher level of being makes it an ideal vehicle for the transmission of food for the soul.

In order to begin you must select a sacred image for which you feel a particular affinity. It will help if the image has its eyes open so that it appears to look back at you. Sit comfortably and place the image so that it is directly in front of you. When you are settled, proceed in the following sequence:

1. Close your eyes and do the Inner Smile exercise.
2. Do the first part of the double breath in order to begin to open your heart center, so that you feel a sense of love and caring for the image.
3. Work on opening the third eye using the conscious breathing and focusing of awareness exercises.
4. Open your eyes and gaze gently into the eyes of the image.
5. Draw the energy that you feel coming from the image into the third eye as you inhale. Let the energy come in and down, working slowly toward the heart center. You can feel the energy flow as a warm and tingling sensation. If you relax,

the experience is unmistakable. If you are not sure whether you feel it, don't be concerned. Keep going and the sensation will clarify itself.

6. The better you do the exercise, the more the image will seem to come to life. It might move, emit colors or sounds. If you are on the right track the image will look back at you.

This exercise should be done for about 20 minutes. The results will vary with the image that you choose, because the nature of the image influences the energy it transmits. As you try different images, this distinction will become clearer. Then you can choose according to your need; either reinforcing an existing attribute or

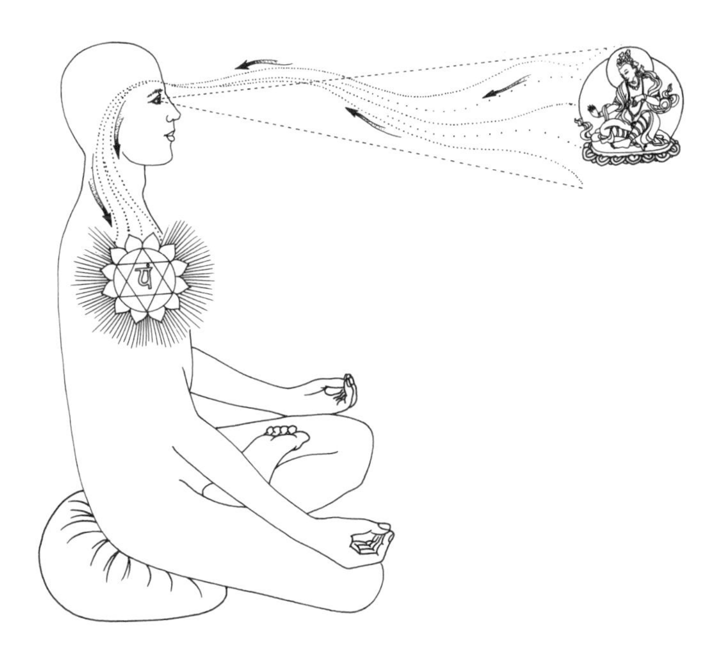

Fig. 51. Draw the energy that you feel from the image into the third eye and then down to the heart center.

picking an image that is strong in a quality that you lack to create a better balance in yourself.

This exercise is similar to the Hindu Puja in which a particular deity is brought to life by the devotee; to the Buddhist meditating on a tanka in order to become one with the deity; or to an Eastern orthodox Christian meditating on an icon, in order to receive its particular vibrations and power. It can be used with any image, but it is most useful with a sacred image that represents a level of being superior to your own, since that ensures that you will receive a higher level of energy.

ADVANCED METHODS

PURIFICATION AND CIRCULATION

Fusion

The design of this experience is based on Taoist traditions, some of which may strike a Westerner as strange or arbitrary. For example, a connection between the ears and the kidneys is not obvious. But it isn't necessary to fully understand the relationship in order to use it. It is sufficient to take an "as if" attitude.

There are two major phases to the fusion process. The first emphasizes the purification and balancing of negative emotions. The second involves the nourishing of the inner system with higher positive qualities. In its complete expression the fusion process works on all three bodies: removing impurities from the physical body; intensifying circulation in the subtle body; and accumulating higher positive qualities that are the expression of the space body.

In order to undertake phase one, certain correspondences between senses, organs, negative emotions, colors and storage areas must be established. These are given in table 6. The process is initiated by connecting the sense (which is externally oriented) with a bodily organ, thereby helping to seal the sense by focusing it inward. It is suggested that as these connections are established between sense and organ, a familiar homecoming feeling will be experienced "like the son and mother meeting again."

Figure 53 gives the location of the bodily organs.

While it is necessary to be clear about these locations in order to be able to proceed, it is even more important to have a physical sensation of their existence and position. This physical sense will become more vivid with practice.

TABLE 6
Correspondences for Fusion Process

	One	Two	Three	Four	Five
Sense Area	Ears	Eyes	Tongue	Mouth	Nose
Organ	Kidneys	Liver	Heart	Spleen	Lungs
Emotion	Fear	Anger	Cruelty	Imbalance	Grief
Color	Blue	Green	Red	Yellow-gold	White
Storage Area	Perineum	3 inches right of belly button	Heart center	Belly button	3 inches left of belly button

Figure 52 is a picture of a Pa Qua that is used to fuse energies and emotions.

The Pa Qua can be built up in the body line by line, but for present purposes it will be sufficient to visualize the total diagram when the necessity arises. At the center of the Pa Qua is a Yin and

Fig. 52. Pa Qua

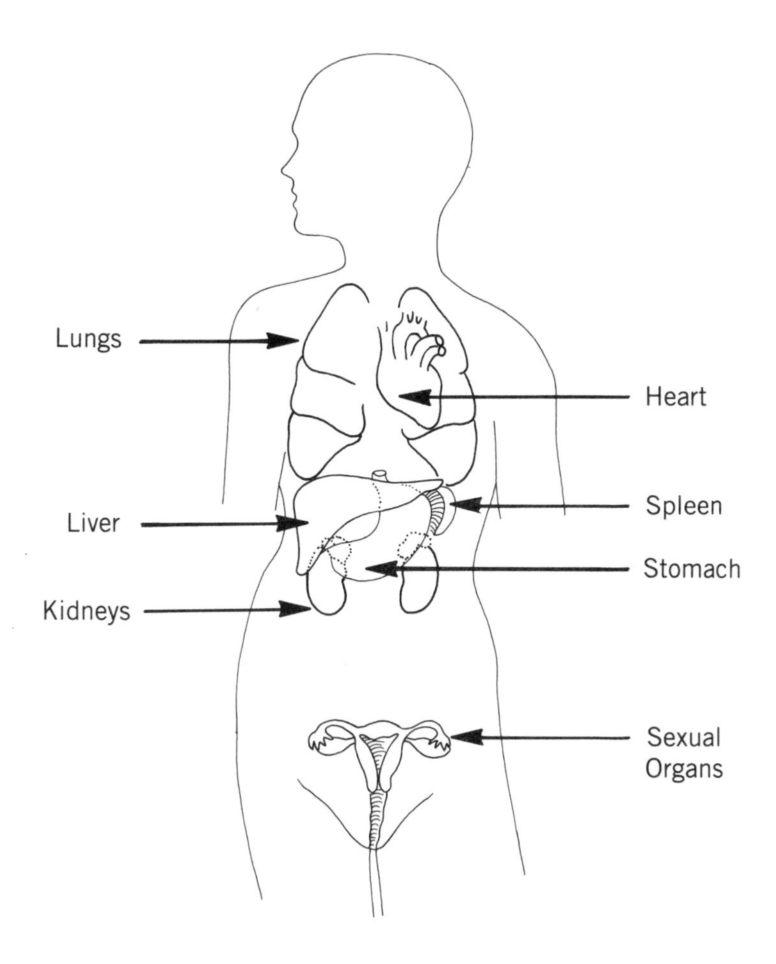

Fig. 53. The organs

Yang, which whirls much like a blender. The energies that are brought to the various storage areas are ultimately brought into the center of the Pa Qua where they are homogenized. After that they are further purified by being circulated down the front line of the body and up the spinal channel, which the Taoists refer to as the microcosmic orbit.

The preceding is an overview of the first part of the fusion process. The following is a more detailed description. Use it systematically. Do not take the next step until the step you are on is fully clear to you:

1. Refer to table 6. Follow the order in which the correspondences are given starting with the ear, kidney, blue, fear connections. Begin by trying to listen to your kidneys. When you have located them in this way, and by referring to figure 53, squeeze out the fear that is stored in them, allowing it to go to the storage point located between the legs in the perineum, visualizing it as a muddy blue.

Proceed with the next four steps summarized in table 6 in exactly the same way from sense, to organ, to storage point. At the conclusion the five negative emotions will have been squeezed out of their respective organs and sent to their storage points.

2. Visualize the Pa Qua pictured in figure 52 being transferred to your belly, placing the middle point on your belly button.
3. Let the spinning Yin and Yang at the center of the Pa Qua draw the energies from the various storage areas (both sides of the belly button, the perineum, and the heart center), and blend them together for 30 seconds in the center of the Pa Qua.
4. Circulate this balanced energy in the microcosmic orbit, down the front line of the body and up the spine at least three times. When you are done, store the energy in the navel, letting it penetrate into the center of the body at that point.

The second phase of the fusion process is a mirror image of the first. Having purged and purified the negative emotions from the organs in which they were stored, their positive complements are returned to the organs in a process known as the "Creative Cycle."

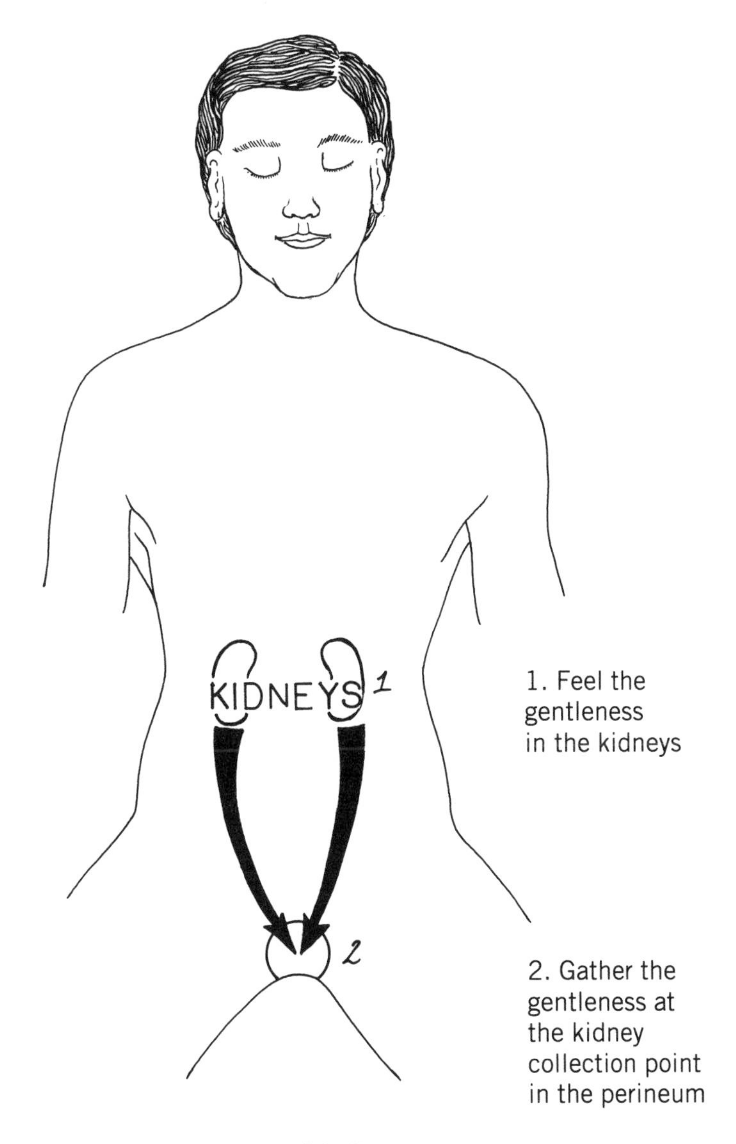

Fig. 54. The first part of the Fusion practice

1. Focus on the kidneys. Sense the gentleness (blue) that is formed there. Let it flow to the collection point in the perineum.

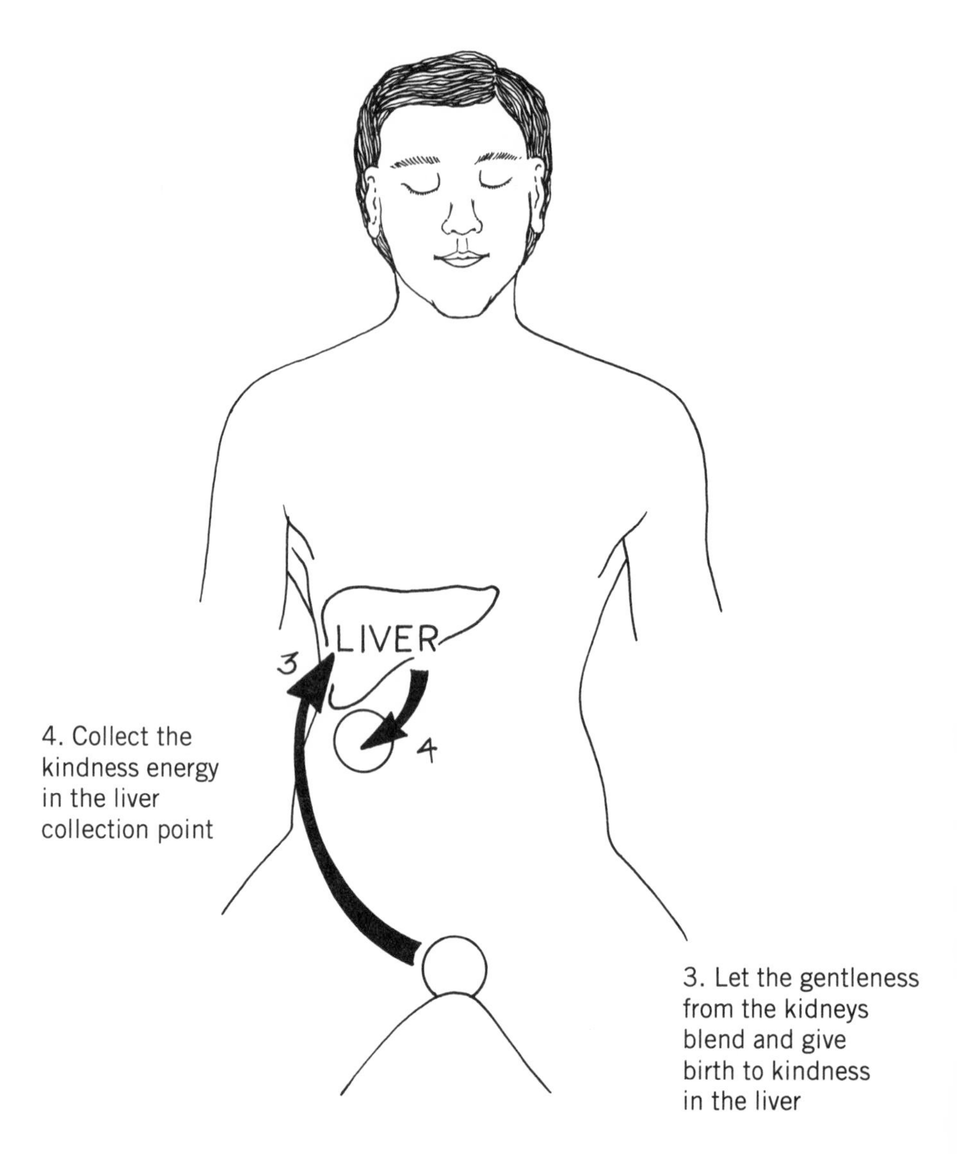

Fig. 55. The second part of the Fusion practice

2. Let this energy go to the liver where it manifests as kindness (green), which overflows gradually into the liver collection point.

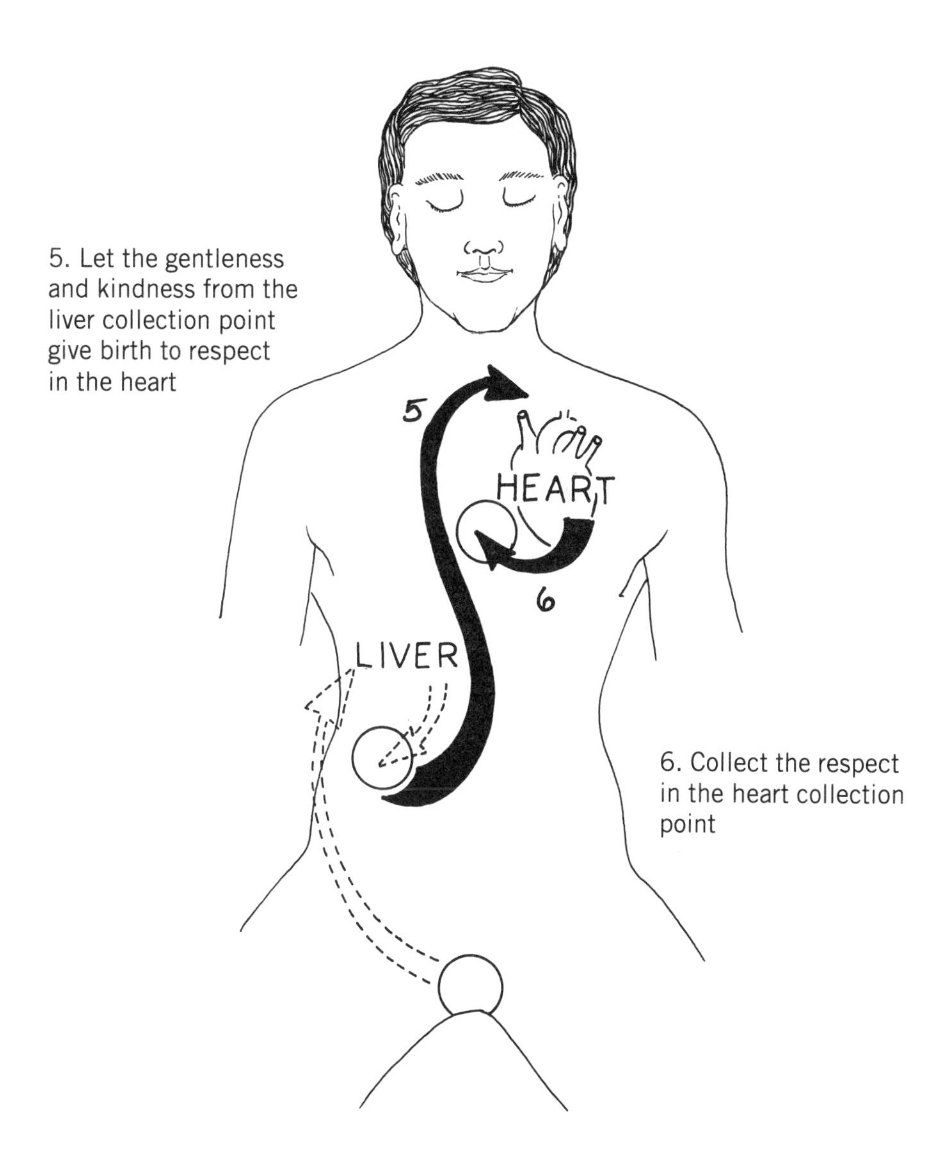

Fig. 56. The third part of the Fusion practice

3. Let this energy flow to the physical heart (red), where it manifests as respect and gradually overflows into the heart collection point.

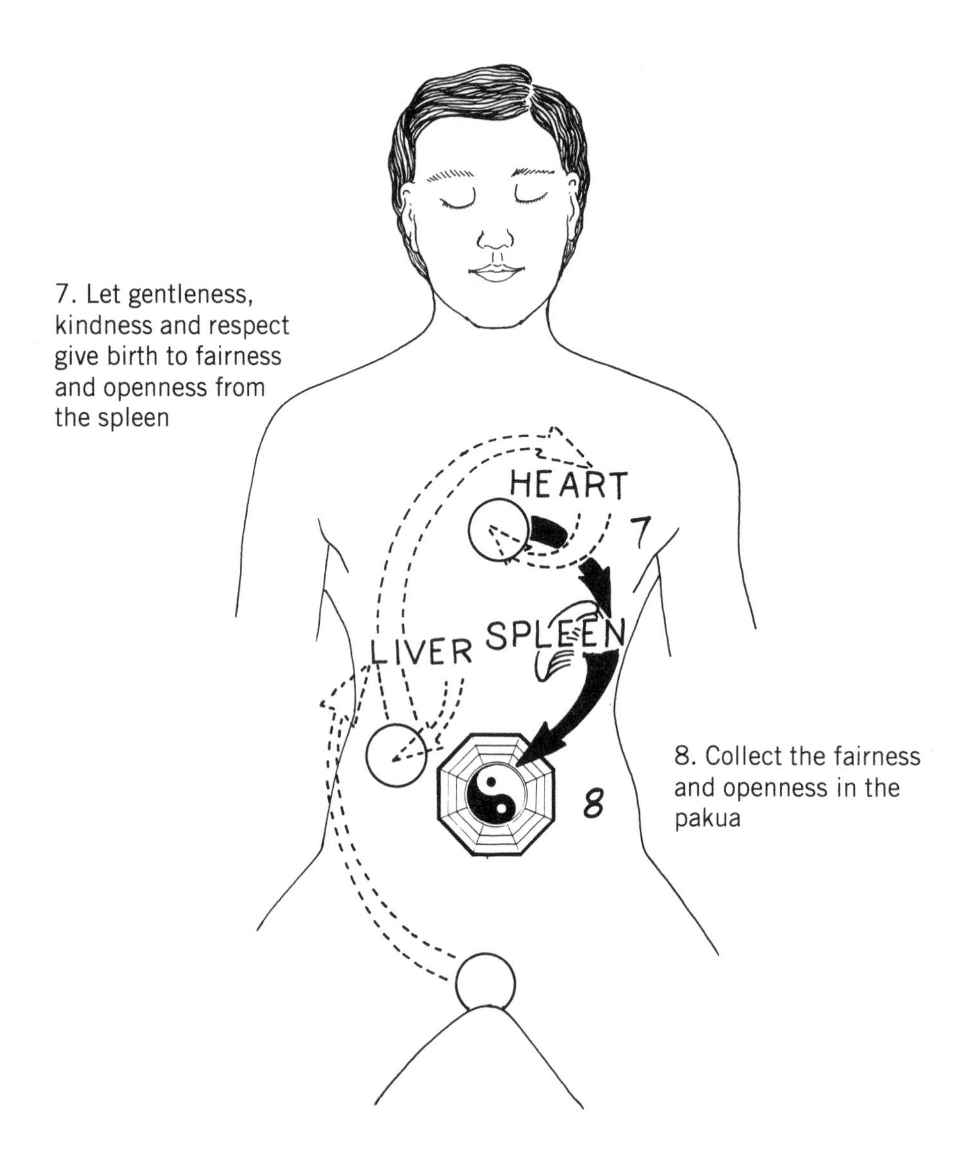

Fig. 57. The fourth part of the Fusion practice

4. Let this energy flow to the spleen (yellowish gold), where it manifests as fairness and equanimity and is gathered in the collection point in the belly in the center of the Pa Qua.

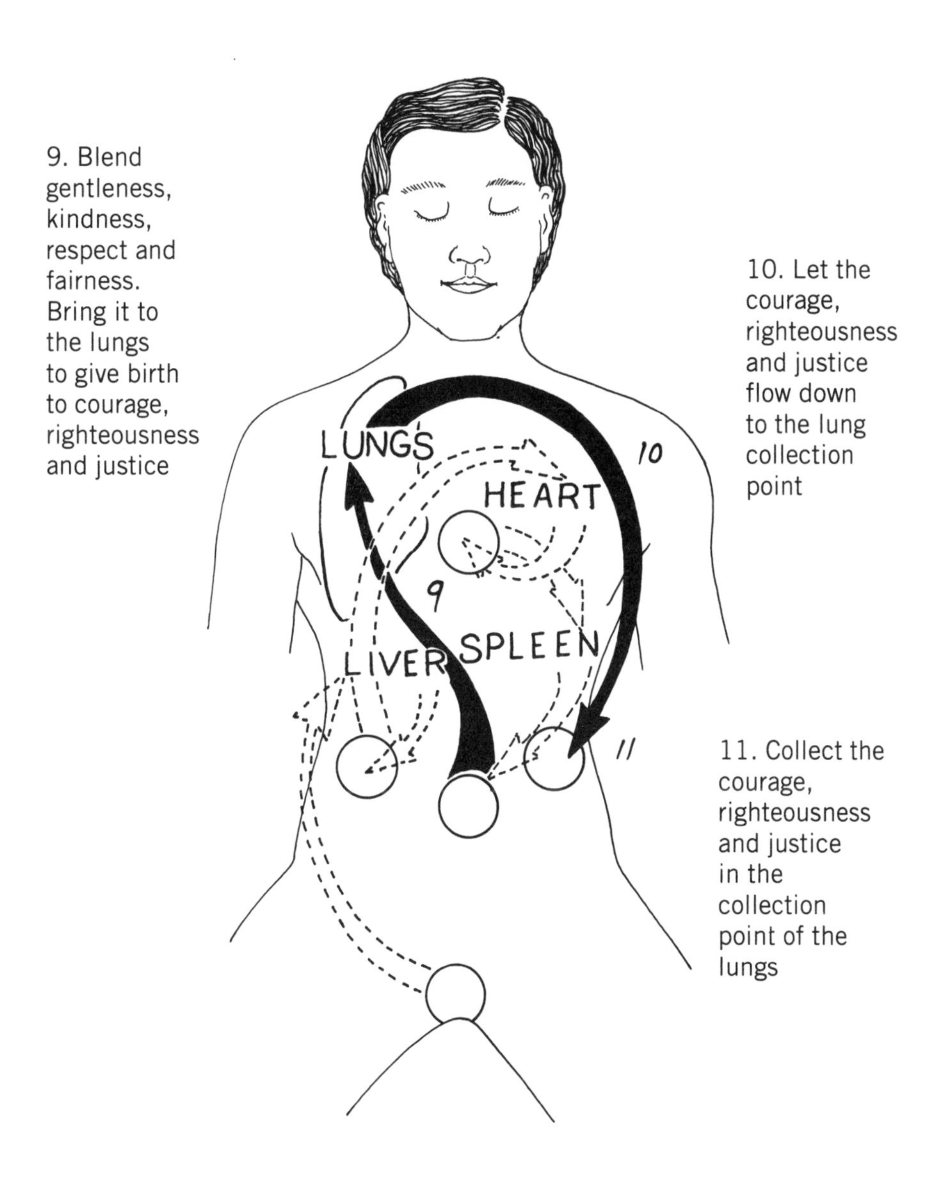

Fig. 58. The fifth part of the Fusion practice

5. Let this energy flow to the lungs (white), where it manifests as dignity and righteousness and is stored in the lung collection point.

6. Repeat the whole cycle two more times ending in the kidney collection point in the perineum.
7. Circulate this energy in the microcosmic orbit at least eight times.
8. Store the refined energy in the core of the body at the level of the belly button.

The color associated with the particular emotional quality is a useful guide to the effectiveness of the process. In the first phase, as the negative emotion is squeezed out of the organ, the color should be murky. In the second phase, as the higher quality is introduced into the organ, the color should be clear and brilliant. If it isn't, the purification is not complete and the step should be worked on further.

Fusion is a subtle and complex process. What is presented above is a highly simplified version. For a more complete explanation see the recent work on the subject by Mantak and Maneewan Chia, *Fusion of the Five Elements I*[9].

OPENING CHAKRAS

The Chakra Animals

The form in which this exercise is given is modern.[10] However, it is based on the widespread and ancient understanding that the chakras are associated with various types of animal energies. In the older systems, such as Hinduism and Buddhism, these associations are traditional. In the present approach the individual discovers the animals associated with particular chakras through spontaneous exploration. This orientation bears some resemblance to the "most secret method" of the Tibetan Buddhists, in which the individual discovers the method that works best for him through creative experimentation.

There are three basic steps to be followed:

1. Prepare for visualization by using any process that helps you relax. The Inner Smile is an appropriate approach.
2. Focus on the forehead. Be aware of any energy or emotional quality that exists in that area. Allow these energies to transform themselves into an animal—it will happen if you let it. Notice what the animal looks like and what it is doing. After a while begin to relate to it. Ask if it has a message for you. Find out its name. At the conclusion of the conversation, thank it for coming and assure it that you will return in the near future.

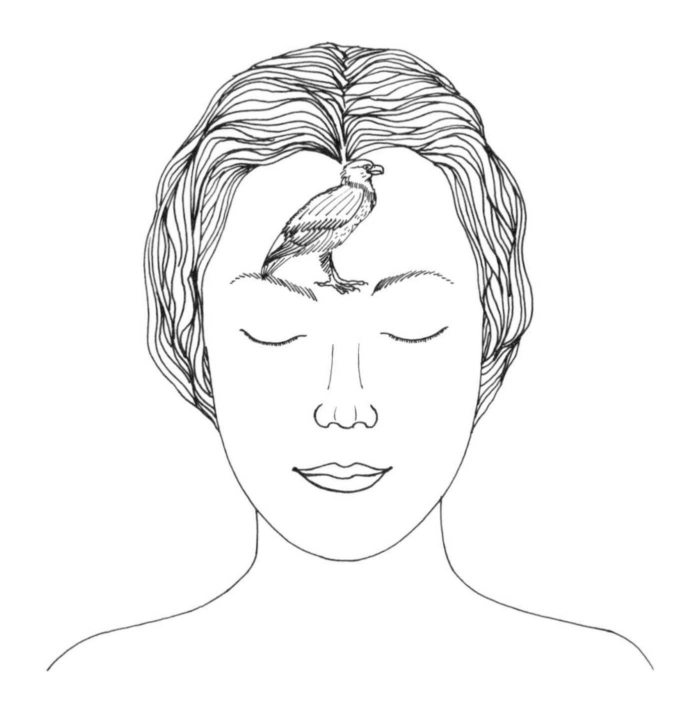

Fig. 59. The animal on the forehead

3. Repeat the process outlined in step two for each of the chakras in turn. Do not hurry! At the conclusion you will have identified an animal associated with each chakra.

This approach belongs to the realm of personal mythology. Unlike many of the previous exercises, it is difficult to predict in advance what will happen. But the more surprising the interaction between you and the animals, the better.

The process described above is just the beginning. It establishes the cast of characters. The next time you do the exercise you can start where you previously left off. See whether the animals have physically changed in any way. Have their concerns altered? Everything about them is charged with personal symbolism and can have a direct impact on the process of personal transformation. It would be helpful to keep a written record of observations on each session so that the pattern of changes will be more evident.

The animals are aspects of your inner world. They should become your friends. They are in a position to explain aspects of yourself that you do not understand, but you have to gain their trust. Then you have to ask them what you need to know. This is a continuing process, like any relationship. Repeat the process once or twice a week for three weeks. Then look back over your notes and you will be in a good position to evaluate its effectiveness.

INTERPERSONAL ASPECTS
Configurations

In any spiritual approach that uses an interpersonal format, it is necessary to consider to whom you are opening. When you sit with another human being, the possibility exists that you may simply exchange poisons, or that you may take something that they need without giving much in return.

The configuration method avoids these problems by creating an intermediate position that acts as a transmitter and receiver of

Fig. 60. Drawing energy from a point in space.

needed energies in the amounts and proportions required. This may sound too good to be true, but experience with a number of individuals in different configurations has suggested both the safety and the effectiveness of this approach.

The configurational approach can be employed with two or more people. If only two, they should sit facing each other. If three, they should sit in a triangle. With more, a circle is natural. Having been seated in an appropriate manner proceed as follows:

1. Each person should put their attention on the center point of the configuration, maintaining only peripheral awareness of the other persons.
2. Continue this process until you feel the center point come alive, as if everyone, including yourself, originated from there. At this stage a bindu has been created through your mutual efforts, from which a mandala has been generated, of which you are a part. Creative energy can radiate from that point in all directions. The center is a doorway to energies from within the earth and beyond the earth as well as from other dimensions. It is a point of manifestation of these ordinarily inaccessible domains, from which each member of the configuration can draw, since they have helped to create it. No one is directly relating to anyone else, so that the difficulties described above do not arise.

A more complete description of this approach will be given in a forthcoming book by one of the authors[11], but what has been presented should be sufficient to enable the reader to begin to explore the approach without waiting for a more elaborate description.

CONCLUSION

You have before you a graded series of practices to utilize in contacting and cultivating your own subtle body. If you use them, these practices will eventually generate a need for something more.

This could take a number of forms: a further book of spiritual exercises; audio and video tapes; workshops providing direct instruction. There are many possibilities. What is essential when you get to that point is to make your needs known. The enclosed postcard is provided for that purpose.

Beyond any of these alternatives is the serious question of whether to follow a particular teacher or teaching. This is the traditional way to study and it contains many advantages if the teacher is good and devoted to the student's growth. But this cannot necessarily be assumed. However, if you feel drawn to a particular way, our advice is to preserve your common sense and mild skepticism as you move forward on whatever path brings you further into the light.

NOTES

PART I
The Subtle Body:
Background, History and Traditions

Chapter One
The Recurrent Image

1. Gunther, Bernard, *Energy Ecstasy*. Los Angeles: Guild of Tutors Press, 1978.
2. *Krishnamurti's Journal*, Ed. By Mary Lutyens, New York: Harper-Row, 1982. See Introduction.
3. Sri Sadhu Om, *The Path Of Sri Ramana* (Part One). Berkeley: Asian Humanities Press, 1981, p. 130.

Chapter Two
The Hindu Tradition

1. Zaehner, R. C. (translator), *Hindi Scriptures*. London: Dent & Sons, 1977, p. 126.
2. Evans-Wentz, W. Y. *Tibetan Yoga And Secret Doctrines.* London: Oxford University Press, 1958.
3. Rama, Swami, *Path Of Fire And Light*. Honesdale: Himalayan Publishers, 1986, p. 129.
4. Woodruff, Sir John. *The Serpent Power*. Madras: Fanesh & Col., 1918.

Chapter Three
Buddhist Systems

1. Ven. Khenpo Karthar, Rinpoche. Personal Communication.

2. Blofeld, John, *The Tantric Mysticism Of Tibet*. New York: E. P. Dutton, 1970.
3. Gyatso, Geshe Kelsang, *Clear Light Of Bliss*. London: Wisdom Publications, 1982.
4. Ibid, p. 23
5. Yogi Chen, C. M., *Discriminations Between Buddhist and Hindu Tantras*. Privately Published. For further information contact Dr. C. T. Shen, 555 Madison Ave., N.Y.C., 10022.
6. Gyatso, Geshe Kelsang, *Clear Light of Bliss*. London: Wisdom Publications, 1982, p. 188.
7. Blofeld, John, *The Tantric Mysticism of Tibet*. New York: E. P. Dutton, 1978, Pps. 189-190.
8. Govinda, Lama A. *Psycho-cosmic Symbolism Of The Buddhist Stupa*. Emeryville: Dharma Publishing, 1976.
9. Gyatso, Geshe Kelsang, *Clear Light of Bliss*. London: Wisdom Publications, 1982.
10. Yogi Chen, C. M., *Discriminations Between Buddhist and Hindu Tantras*. Privately Published.
11. Govinda, Lama A., *Foundations Of Tibetan Mysticism*. New York: Weiser, 1974.
12. Namgyal, Rinpoche, *The Womb Of Form*. Ottawa: Crystal Work Publications, 1981.
13. Gyatso, Geshe Kelsang, *Clear Light of Bliss*. London: Wisdom Publications, 1982, Pps. 22-23.
14. Clifford, Terry, *Tibetan Buddhist Medicine and Psychiatry*. New York: Weiser, 1984.

Chapter Four
The Taoist Approach

1. Yutang, Lin. *The Wisdom of China and India*. New York: Random House, 1942, p. 583.
2. Wilhelm, Richard, (translator) *The Secret Of The Golden Flower*. New York: Brace & World, 1967.
3. Ibid, p. 34.
4. Chia, Mantak, *Taoist Ways To Transform Stress Into Vitality*: The Inner Smile. Huntington: Healing Tao Press, 1985.

5. Huang Ti.
6. Luk, Charles, *Taoist Yoga*. York Beach: Weiser, 1973.
7. Chia, Mantak & Maneewan, *Fusion of Five Elements*, 1 & 2. Huntington, L. I., Healing Tao Center. 1983.

Chapter Five
Other Traditions

1. Annon., "Human Vital Force In Other Systems." *The Psychic Observer & Chimes*. Vol. XXXV111 No. 3, Oct-Dec., 1978, 241-242.
2. Katz, R., "Education For Transcendence: Lessons from the Kung Zhu Twasi." *Journal of Transpersonal Psychology*, November, 2, 1973.
3. Harvey Wasserman, Personal Communication.
4. Waters, Frank. *Pumpkin Seed Point*. Chicago: Sage Books, 1969, p. 139.
5. Charles Lawrence, Personal Communication.
6. Ferguson, George. *Signs and Symbols In Christian Art*. New York: Oxford Press, 1954.
7. French, R. M. (translator) *The Way Of A Pilgrim*. New York: Seabury Press, 1970.
8. Cayce, Edgar, *A Commentary On The Book Of The Revelation*. Virginia Beach: A.R.E. Press, 1970.
9. Ouspensky, P.D. *In Search Of The Miraculous*. New York: Harcourt Brace, 1949, p. 102.
10. For example: "The Lost Gospel Of Jesus: The Hidden Teachings Of Christ." (*The Sacred Teachings of Light*, Codex V111 Ser.) XV, 91p, 1984.
11. Cartwright, Fairfax, L. Sir, *The Mystic Rose From The Garden Of The King*. London: Watkins, 1976.
12. Fortune, Dion, *The Mystical Qabalah*. York Beach: Weiser, 1984.

Chapter Six
Conclusions

1. Neff, Dio Urmilla, "The Great Chakra Controversy." *Yoga Journal*, Nov-Dec., 1985
2. Durckheim, K. G., *Hara: The Vital Centre Of Man*. London: Unwin Paperbacks, 1977.
3. Gyatso, Geshe Kelsang, *Clear Light Of Bliss*. London: Wisdom Publications, 1982.
4. Chia, Mantak, *Iron Shirt Chi Kung I*. Huntington, L. I., Healing Tao Books, 1986.
5. Gyatso, Geshe Kelsang. *Clear Light of Bliss*. New York: Wisdom Publications, 1982.
6. Luk, Charles, *Taoist Yoga*. York Beach: Weiser, 1973.
7. Jung, C. G. "The Psychology Of Transference." In *Collected Works* Vol. 16. New York: Pantheon Books, Pps. 163-326.

PART II
Awakening the Subtle Body

1. Chia, Mantak *Taoist Ways To Transfrom Stress Into Vitality*: The Inner Smile. Huntington: Healing Tao Press, 1985.
2. The control of attention is at the heart of most meditative practices. Conscious breathing, as given in this exercise, is a generic form of Pranayama Yoga upon which more specializeed breathing exercises can be built.
3. Rudrananda, Swami, *The Nature Of Spiritual Work*. Big Indian, New York: RBIC Press, 1988, p. 10-11.
4. Garrison, Omar. *Tantra: The Yoga Of Sex*. New York: Causeway Books, 1964.
5. Blofeld, John. *The Tantric Mysticism of Tibet*. New York: E. P. Dutton, 1970, Pps. 150-163.
6. Prayer is found in virtually all religious traditions. The use of visualization is also widely employed. Its most detailed expression is probably found in Tantric Buddhism where the imagry to be visualized may take 5 - 10 pages to describe.

7. Moum, Margaret R., "The Ha Rite." *Psychic Observer & Chimes*, Vol. XXXV111 # 3, 232-237.
8. Religious Art is created to act as a transmitter for spiritual energy. In relating to such art one needs to be in an open and surrendered state. Russian Icons are a good example of this type of art. They are typically approached through prayer and devotion.
9. Chia, Mantak & Maneewan, *Fusion of the Five Elements I.* Huntington, L. I.: Healing Tao Books, 1989.
10. Gallegos, Eligio S. "Animal Imagry, The Chakra System And Psychotherapy." *Journal Of Transpersonal Psychology*, 1983, Vol. 15, No. 2, pp. 125-135.
11. Mann, J. H. *Configurational Tantra.* (in preparation).

INDEX

GLOBE PRESS BOOKS

Order Form / Mailing List Request

How to order:
Payment must accompany order. Please remember to calculate shipping charges according to the Shipping chart. For shipment to addresses in New York State, please add appropriate sales tax. Mail the completed order form (or a copy) with your payment to Globe Press Books at the address below. *Foreign Orders:* Surface shipping takes 2-15 weeks. Checks must be American Express or international checks drawn on a U.S. Bank. *Mailing List:* Simply fill in the name and address portion of the order form and return it to the address below.

Qty.	Title	Price	Total
		Subtotal	
		Tax	
		Shipping	
		Total	

SHIPPING CHARGES

	Surface	Air
U.S.A.	$1.75 first item, .50 each addtl.	$3.50 first item, 1.00 each addtl.
Canada & Mexico	$3.00 first item, 1.00 each addtl.	$4.50 first item, 2.00 each addtl.
Europe	$3.00 first item, 1.00 each addtl.	$8.50 first item, 3.00 each addtl.
Southern Hemisphere	$3.00 first item, 1.00 each addtl.	$10.00 first item, 5.75 each addtl.

Our Guarantee
Return any book in saleable condition within 30 days for a prompt and friendly refund.

Name ______________________________

Address ______________________________

____

City / State / Zip ______________________________

Country / Postcode ______________________________

Mail to: Globe Press Books, P.O. Box 2045-B, Madison Square Station, New York, NY 10159. *Thank you for your order.*